Whatever you do at
work & in life :
MAKE IT MATTER!

MAKE IT MATTER

MAKE IT MATTER

How Managers Can Motivate
by Creating Meaning

Scott Mautz

AMACOM

American Management Association

New York • Atlanta • Brussels • Chicago • Mexico City • San Francisco
Shanghai • Tokyo • Toronto • Washington, D.C.

Bulk discounts available. For details visit:
www.amacombooks.org/go/specialsales
Or contact special sales:
Phone: 800-250-5308
E-mail: specialsls@amanet.org
View all the AMACOM titles at: www.amacombooks.org
American Management Association: www.amanet.org

This publication is designed to provide accurate and authoritative information in regard to the subject matter covered. It is sold with the understanding that the publisher is not engaged in rendering legal, accounting, or other professional service. If legal advice or other expert assistance is required, the services of a competent professional person should be sought.

LIBRARY OF CONGRESS CATALOGING-IN-PUBLICATION DATA
Mautz, Scott.
  Make it matter : how managers can motivate by creating meaning /
Scott Mautz.—1 Edition.
    pages cm
  Includes index.
  ISBN 978-0-8144-3617-2 (hardcover)—ISBN 0-8144-3617-X (hardcover)—ISBN
978-0-8144-3618-9 (e-book)—ISBN 0-8144-3618-8 (e-book) 1. Leadership.
2. Employee motivation. 3. Meaning (Psychology) I. Title.
  HD57.7.M3935 2015
  658.3'14—dc23

  2014042342

About AMA
American Management Association (www.amanet.org) is a world leader in talent development, advancing the skills of individuals to drive business success. Our mission is to support the goals of individuals and organizations through a complete range of products and services, including classroom and virtual seminars, webcasts, webinars, podcasts, conferences, corporate and government solutions, business books, and research. AMA's approach to improving performance combines experiential learning—learning through doing—with opportunities for ongoing professional growth at every step of one's career journey.

Printing number

10 9 8 7 6 5 4

CONTENTS

Introduction

WHEN THE NOBEL PRIZE–WINNING PHYSICIST RICHARD FEYNMAN was still getting his graduate degree at Princeton, he was asked to oversee a group of engineers who were tasked, without much context, to perform an endless series of tedious calculations. The math wasn't especially difficult if you were an engineer, but the work proceeded very slowly and it was full of errors. Growing more frustrated with the performance, Feynman made a critical discovery that would dramatically alter the course of events moving forward. He realized the problem wasn't the math, but that the engineers were totally disengaged. So he sagely convinced his superiors to let the engineers in on what he already knew—why they were performing the calculations, and why they were sweating their tails off in the New Mexico desert—in Los Alamos, New Mexico, to be exact.

It was at that time that Feynman's boss, Robert Oppenheimer, pierced the veil of secrecy that had surrounded the work and let the engineers in on the enormity of what they were doing. They weren't simply doing routine math for some inconsequential lab exercise. They were performing calculations that would enable them to complete the race to build the atomic bomb before the Germans did.

Their work would win the war.

The workplace, the work, and the workers' performance were completely transformed once the task was imbued with meaning. From that point forward, Feynman reported that the scientists worked ten times faster than before with few mistakes, and with fierce commitment.[1]

Meaning matters.

Obviously, not every workplace has as meaningful a backdrop as global conflict. However, this book will show you what's possible in any place of work, in *your* place of work, when meaning-rich experiences are facilitated and the resultant energy is channeled toward work that truly matters.

Engagement and productivity would know no limits—and that's something we need more than ever.

One of the great business conundrums of our time is working with shrinking budgets and compressed timelines but inflated demands for productivity. We're working harder and longer for less and without a lot of conviction. The statistics don't lie; in this increasingly more with less business world, a shocking number of workers are more or less disengaged. Our potential is slipping away along with, most likely, our profits.

For the well-meaning manager, there is a solution to this conundrum, one that can transcend the typical short-term fixes, inspire growth and fulfillment, unlock sustained effort, and give everyone a greater return on their investment in time at work.

It's *meaning*.

This book teaches you how to motivate by creating meaning *so that everyone profits*—the company and all of its constituents.

Perhaps you're thinking that meaning is just a higher-order concept, nice to imagine but too ethereal and touchy-feely to have any practical application.

Make It Matter will shatter that misconception with dozens of proven exercises, tools, and instructions. You'll find provocative, insightful new concepts for driving the highest level of sustained performance in your organization while unlocking deep fulfillment for your constituents (and yourself) along the way.

This book is meant for managers looking to step up, stand out, and make a step change by reframing and reinvigorating a work life that so many want so much more from. It's for those who want to work with a clear and rewarding sense of purpose and who want their work to amount to a compelling legacy left behind. It's for those who want to motivate truly peak performance. And it's for those who want to inspire and improve the whole lives of those reporting to them, not just the eight hours they're together.

part one

DEFINITION

CHAPTER 1

Why Meaning Matters

DO YOU MATTER AT WORK?

The question isn't do you earn your paycheck, or are you good at what you do.

Do . . . you . . . matter?

Does the work you do uniquely make a difference to your company and to others—and does it matter *to you*?

Far too many of us feel our hours at work don't count. While our plates may seem full, our lives may not. As a result, many of us simply disengage at some level. Gallup research found that 71 percent of American workers can be coded as either "not engaged" or "actively disengaged" in their work, meaning they are emotionally disconnected from their workplaces and are less likely to be productive.[1] "Actively disengaged" can even mean that workers are undermining their workplace environment with negative attitudes and behaviors that amount to sabotage (we've probably all run into at least one of these people).

Other studies on workplace engagement have come to similar conclusions. The Conference Board's 2014 survey indicates that only 47.7 percent of Americans are satisfied with their jobs, down from 61.1 percent when the survey was first conducted in 1987, and a study by the

BlessingWhite research company showed alarming disengagement levels in workplaces around the world. Towers Watson further indicated that "businesses appear to be at a critical tipping point in their ability to maintain engagement over time."[2]

Surely, though, at the highest levels of a company, the executive level, where salaries are stratospheric in some cases, the problem of disengagement doesn't exist, right?

Not the case. While engagement does increase as you move higher up the company chain, a full 41 percent of those at the executive level cannot be coded as engaged, according to BlessingWhite. The impact on the workplace is obviously detrimental: As the report points out, "One dead battery will not jump-start another."[3]

Surely, this problem exists primarily among the less educated workers, those with a high school diploma or less who are making less money or might be laboring in less stimulating jobs—right?

Again, this is not the case. Those with at least some college education are significantly *less* likely to be engaged in their jobs than are those with a high school diploma or less.[4]

Surely the problem exists primarily in smaller companies that don't have the financial resources to combat the sense of malaise, true?

This is another misconception. Leigh Branham and Mark Hirschfeld, authors of *Re-Engage*, found a direct correlation between company size and engagement—the larger the company size the *lower* the level of reported engagement.[5] While smaller employers still suffer from disengagement issues, they are better able to maintain the connective power between the rank and file than companies that have grown substantially in number of employees.

The problem of a disengaged workforce is more widespread than most of us would dream possible. Which means the existence of workplaces that are barren of meaning is more widespread than anyone would care to admit. And when meaning in our work is absent, we tend to disengage at some level.

The provision of meaning is the solution for disengagement.

In fact, William Kahn, professor of organizational behavior at Boston University, has drawn a direct link between meaningfulness and engagement.

Kahn conducted a study among counselors/instructors at an adolescent summer camp in the West Indies, seeking to understand the conditions in which people psychologically engage or disengage in work.[6] Kahn's theory was that people make choices to input or withdraw degrees of themselves in their work roles. In general, people like to bring their preferred selves into their roles. He described a scuba instructor camp counselor who put great energy and care into instructing students to dive and who experienced a deep sense of personal engagement. The scuba instructor had chosen to invest physically ("darting about checking gear and leading the dive"), cognitively ("with vigilant awareness" of his divers, the weather, and marine life), and emotionally ("in empathizing with the fear and excitement of the young divers"). He expressed himself and his love of the ocean (and desire for others to love it as well) by talking about the wonders of the ocean, steering boat drivers toward minimally invasive routes around vulnerable coral reefs, and showing his playfulness and joy underwater. The instructor connected with others and with a task that deeply tapped what was important to him, and in so doing he was expressing a preferred self.

This scuba instructor contrasted with a highly disengaged windsurfing instructor who had withdrawn physically (sending students out and "just laying around"), cognitively ("not telling them much or helping them out much"), and emotionally ("being bland, superficial, and talking in unemotional tones").[7] The windsurfing instructor's withdrawal and disengagement kept her from connecting with others and the task at hand in a manner that was congruent with the expression of her preferred self.

Why such a stark difference between the level of engagement of the two instructors?

It came down to the absence or presence of meaning in the work.

Kahn discovered three psychological conditions that drove people to engage, expressed as three questions that people seem to subconsciously ask themselves before choosing whether to fully engage. Two of these questions speak to very basic human needs. The first: How safe is it for me to personally engage—that is, are there negative consequences to self-image, status, or career for personally engaging? The second question: Am I available to engage—do I have the physical and emotional energy to personally engage, distraction-free? The third question was by far the most important and powerful: How meaningful is it for me to bring myself into this task—and will I receive a personal return on investment?[8]

Therein lies a fundamental human truth. Christopher Bartlett from Harvard Business School has said, "People don't come to work to be number one or number two, or to get 20 percent return on assets; they come to work to get *meaning* from their lives."[9] They come to work looking to get a very personal return on investment.

In fact, *70 percent of us* are experiencing a greater search for meaning at work than in life.[10] And when work has meaning it drives the expenditure and investment of discretionary energy on a physical, cognitive, and emotional level. The investor enjoys a personal return, a feeling. It's the feeling that you matter and are making a difference; your engagement is paying off.

Sadly, too many people aren't investing enough of their energy to yield a decent return for themselves, their company, or anyone. It is the direct effect of a crisis of meaning.

A shocking number of people sadly accept their fate at work. They are effectively quitting and staying—settling for a paycheck, abandoning hope of finding fulfillment in their jobs, and knowing in their heart of hearts that they aren't performing anywhere near their maximum potential.

So we try throwing money at the problem. We ask for more pay in an attempt to get the feeling of emptiness to subside, and maybe we get it. But it's not that simple (as we all intuitively know). If all it took was money, then lottery winners would stop working. However, a pool of sociological research known as "The Lottery Studies" indicates the exact opposite; the large majority of big lottery winners choose to keep working.[11] The daily pursuit of meaning at work is a powerful draw. More powerful than the draw of a lotto-ball, it turns out.

Managers with the best intentions try a variety of tactics to ultimately elevate performance. We staff up. We spend more on technology to get better, cheaper, faster performance. We cut costs and corners to squeeze out better financial performance. We invest in better surroundings, better workplace facilities.

And yet a lack of engagement and fulfillment in the workplace rages on.

So employees try to take it into their own hands. Perhaps they drift into the bookstore with a gnawing sense that something is missing in their work lives. They line up to spend their hard-earned money for wisdom on how to elevate their game, how to get their mojo back. They are faced with a wall of mastery books cajoling them to Lead Better! Execute Better! Innovate Better! Or perhaps they attend a training or seminar here and there looking for a dose of inspiration. And perhaps one of these mechanisms helps, for a little while.

But it doesn't last. And so the void of fulfillment and disappearance of personal excellence accordingly follow suit. This absence of meaning can lead to resignation and withdrawal. Given that adults spend more than half their waking life at work, we deserve better.

We deserve something that matters. We deserve something with resonance. We deserve meaning.

Simply put, meaning is *the* performance enhancer of our times. And by the way, it's free.

THE MEANING OF "MEANING"

So what is meant by the word *meaning,* anyway?

We find meaning (or meaningfulness) in things that make emotional connections and are remembered, and thus matter.[12] When we feel belongingness or a sense that we are cared for, for example, it's meaningful. We also find meaning in things that make us feel significant, that help us reach our full potential, that help us make sense of things, and that serve who we are and what's most important to us.

It is critical to note that, as organizational experts Michael Pratt (Boston College) and Blake Ashforth (Arizona State) have discerned, meaning can be derived *in* and *at* work.[13] As human beings, we can find significance and fulfillment in the work itself depending on the impact it has on who and what is important to us and its congruence with who we are. When we find a significant "to do" in our work—when we feel we are making a real impact on business results and positively affecting the lives of others, are doing work consistent with our values and beliefs, and are able to invest in our betterment every day—it matters. It helps us make sense of ourselves and why we do what we do. It helps answer the soul-searching questions: Why am I here? Who am I? and What's the point?[14]

In this way, we find meaning *in* work.

As humans, we also long for connection to others and an environment that feels like a community. When we have a great sense of belongingness at work—when we feel that work is a place where we can express our true, best selves every day, and feel a tremendous sense of connectedness and harmony with our coworkers, leaders, and organization—it matters. It helps us make sense of the surrounding environment and our place within it, which also helps answer the questions, Who am I? and Where do I belong?[15]

In this way, we find meaning *at* work.

Make It Matter will address how to facilitate the creation of meaning both in and at work in ways that deeply engage the mind, heart, and soul and that elevate performance to new levels.

MEANING AS A COMPETITIVE ADVANTAGE

When it comes to elevating performance to unprecedented levels and creating competitive advantage, meaning really matters.

McKinsey consultants Susie Cranston and Scott Keller have been conducting research with management executives for over a decade to discover the key drivers of absolute peak performance. What have they found?

Nothing contributes more to peak performance than having a personal stake in something. They labeled this phenomenon the Meaning Quotient (MQ) of work. Executives stated that employees at their peak of performance, driven by a meaning-rich work environment, were five times more productive than they usually were. Furthermore, more than 90 percent of executives identified the bottlenecks to peak performance in their organizations as meaning-related issues.[16]

More than a hundred studies have now found that the most engaged employees—those who report they are fully invested in their jobs, committed to their employers, and are working in meaning-rich workplaces—are significantly more productive, drive higher customer satisfaction, and outperform those who are less engaged.[17]

And yet Gallup has cited that disengaged employees working in meaning-bare work environments cost the American economy up to $350 billion per year in lost productivity.[18] That's a lot of disengaged and disenfranchised employees laboring in meaningless conditions.

So where's the breakdown? Why aren't managers connecting the dots?

It starts with helping managers fully comprehend the crisis of meaning in the workplace today and helping them understand the potential for serious competitive advantage by facilitating meaning in and at work.

Statistics abound that illustrate the link between highly engaged, meaning-rich workplaces and top- and bottom-line results. For example:

* Companies with highly engaged employees demonstrate a three-year revenue growth of 20.1 percent (compared to the 8.9 percent that their industry peers will average) and generate three-year earnings growth three times higher than their industry peers.[19]

* In companies where 60 percent to 70 percent of employees were engaged, average total shareholder's return (TSR) stood at 24.2 percent; in companies with only 49 percent to 60 percent of their employees engaged, TSR fell to 9.1 percent; companies with engagement rates below 25 percent suffered negative TSR.[20]

* Companies with high sustaining engagement had an average

one-year operating margin of 27 percent, 2.7 times higher than companies with low engagement levels.[21]

✳ Companies with higher-than-average employee engagement also had 27 percent higher profits, 50 percent higher sales, and 50 percent higher customer loyalty.[22]

✳ Companies that land on Fortune's list of the Best Companies to Work For are invariably characterized by a multitude of attributes that facilitate meaning in the workplace. A 2011 study showed their stock performed three times better than the S&P 500 between 1997 and 2011.[23]

Meaning also has a huge impact on retention, a critical factor should a shortage of talented labor arise in the coming years, as many pundits believe will happen. The BlessingWhite study indicated among those employees coded as "engaged," 81 percent intended to stay at their jobs for at least the next twelve months, in stark contrast to the disengaged, of which only 23 percent intended to stay. This same study astutely noted that "the engaged stay for what they can give, the disengaged for what they can get."[24]

Any company interested in upping retention would want to be considered a top workplace; reputation helps drive retention. Doug Claffey, CEO of Workplace Dynamics, which surveys more than 5,000 companies a year, says that employees in top-rated workplaces, regardless of industry or profession, most importantly can answer yes to the question: Do you feel your work is meaningful?[25] Providing meaningful work will also be of paramount importance to attracting and retaining millennials, who will make up half the workforce in the coming years. It is well known that millennials are not as concerned with money and benefits as their parents were, and that they are much more concerned about whether they have found truly meaningful work. Competitive advantage can't be maintained if you can't hire and retain the bodies to maintain it.

Facilitating meaning breeds competitive advantage by bringing out our personal best as well. When our work gives us meaning it gives us perspective. We are quickly able to recast the lows we experience from the less nourishing parts of our working lives as necessary but temporary sidebars to the main act of making a difference in things that matter most to us. It helps us to quickly put failures and setbacks behind us and reframe their significance because we know there are other enriching, mission-critical tasks to attend to. When we feel lost, meaning gives us something to return to.

Meaning also helps us understand why we are working so hard—and to what end. Meaningful work coaxes the expenditure of more and more discretionary energy out of us and encourages greater risk taking, manifesting itself not only in peak performance but greater personal development as well.

PROFOUND PERFORMANCE

The fact is that facilitating meaning not only drives employees to engage, but takes them beyond engagement to elevated performance and true fulfillment. This is critical because many things can capture an employee's time, attention, and engagement, temporarily. Meaning holds the engagement at the deepest, most fulfilling level, and it *sustains over the long haul*, constantly flowing back into a virtuous cycle of deeper engagement, more meaning, deeper fulfillment, and ever-escalating performance.

I call this phenomenon *profound performance*.

It's the *depth* and *duration* of engagement and fulfillment that accompanies the *height* of the associated performance that makes it profound. It is an absolute competitive advantage in the market for those managers and manufacturers that can create it.

And it is the inspiring end-goal for those managers who want to make work matter.

MEANING AS A
COMPASSIONATE ADVANTAGE

So the evidence that facilitating meaning in the workplace can lead to competitive advantage is clear. Harvard professors Rakesh Khurana and Joel Podolny indicate that there is more to it, however: "We believe there is a connection between meaning creation and performance. Meaning can be the foundation of sustainable competitive advantage. Our only concern is that the significance of meaning creation not be subordinated to a concern with performance. Meaning creation is too important as an end in and of itself."[26]

Said another way, facilitating meaning is just the right thing to do. It's how managers can give others a *compassionate advantage*. When all is said and done, if given the means and opportunity, why wouldn't we endeavor to create a truly fulfilling workplace environment for our fellow human beings? Why not have the compassion and consideration to make the lives of others as enriching and meaningful as possible?

At the most fundamental level, we all crave meaning in our lives. It cannot be underestimated just how deep this desire runs. To have meaning in our lives is at the core of what it means to be a human being. To have meaning is to sort through our 24/7 workload and mounting stress and suddenly have comprehension—an understanding of why we are here on this earth and an understanding of who we are and that what we do matters. A deep and quiet joy accompanies this understanding. Why not give others every advantage we can at work toward enabling a deeply happier life?

And by the way, facilitating the derivation of meaning for others will be deeply meaningful for you, too.

CHAPTER 2

The Markers of Meaning

MANY PEOPLE ASSUME THEY CAN NEVER FIND MEANING IN THEIR work. Meaning is something you find outside the office: in your family, in your church, in your community, in your personal pursuits—things that are your choice, not someone else's. As to the few who do find meaning from 9 to 5, lucky them. They've stumbled on a task that makes their heart sing. They've been pulled into friendships that transcend the office. They've learned new capabilities that have reshaped their view of themselves. Meaning really found them.

In truth, finding meaning in and at work doesn't have to be happenstance. You can create it because meaning is derived from seven specific conditions that I call the *Markers of Meaning*. Satisfy these conditions and you create meaning and fulfillment for yourself and your employees. Profound performance will soon follow suit.

I identified the seven Markers of Meaning by poring through hundreds of sociological, psychological, and organizational behavior studies from top universities and other sources, including statistical modeling that incorporates millions of employee data points gathered in a massive workplace performance study.[1] In addition, I used scores of interviews, including wisdom from over thirty CEOs and executive officers, who provide a top-down point of view; the grassroots perspective from gifted managers at a balance of small and big companies recognized as great places to work; and the perspective from talented managers at nontraditional workplaces.[2] All of this data is complemented by two decades of personal experience from my interactions with thousands of course participants, consulting clients, and keynote attendees.

The Markers of Meaning can be organized within three groupings, as shown in Table 2-1: (1) conditions that yield a calming and clarifying sense of inner Direction, (2) conditions that lead to a gratifying sense of self-Discovery and growth, and (3) conditions that engender Devotion to one's work and a deeper connection between employer, employees, and a greater good. Let's consider them group by group.

Table 2-1. *The Markers of Meaning (conditions creating meaning* in *and* at *work).*

Direction	1. Doing work that matters (significant work that makes a real impact on you/the business/others and is reflective of your values and beliefs, and worthy of your focus and energy)
Discovery	2. Being congruently challenged (in ways that personally energize and maximize individual learning and growth) 3. Working with a heightened sense of competency and self-esteem (feeling valued and valuable, worthy and worthwhile) 4. Being in control and influencing decisions/outcomes (sense of autonomy)
Devotion	5. Working in a caring/authentic/teamwork-based culture (feeling appreciated; being able to bring one's whole self to work; having a sense of belongingness and harmony with coworkers, leaders, and company) 6. Feeling connection with and confidence in leadership and the mission (sensing you fit within the mission and can make a difference toward that mission) 7. Being free from corrosive workplace behaviors (removing barriers to the best self)

DIRECTION

Three short words, presented as a question, can encapsulate our frustration and depth of emptiness at work:

What's the point?

When we can't answer this question about what we are doing, we lose our commitment. Our time feels wasted, and so do we. We lose our bearings. How did we become so disconnected from doing something that counts?

It really matters when the work we are doing doesn't.

There may be no greater driver of meaning in the workplace than work that is purposeful and significant—to the individual and others affected by the work.[3] Doing work that matters is the first and most fundamental Marker of Meaning.

When our work has a point, it justifies and even explodes the expenditure of our time and energy. When our work reflects our values and beliefs, it feels important and promotes a sense of inner harmony. When we are doing work that matters, it provides a sense of inner direction and helps to guide our thoughts, behaviors, actions, and reactions.

Yale's Amy Wrzesniewski, a professor of organizational behavior, has shown that humans are most deeply fulfilled and energized when work is congruent with our innermost direction—that is, when we are doing work that is deeply significant to us and others and, ideally, when it feels like what we were meant to do. In fact, her research shows that people have three distinct orientations toward their work. They consider it a job, a career, or a calling.

Those who relate to their work as a job see it for the material gain they get from the job: the money, benefits, and general means for making a living and having the resources needed to enjoy their lives outside of work. The things that most hold their interest and passion are not found within their work.

Those who view their work as a career are much more involved in their occupation, seeing it as a chance for monetary reward but also as a chance to advance in the organizational structure. This positional advancement brings greater social status, more power within the work-place, and greater self-esteem.

And those who view their work as a calling see their work and life as highly intertwined and inseparable.[4] While financial reward may or may not come with the work, the primary connective tissue that binds these individuals to their work is the deep sense of fulfillment they derive from it.

The research showed that those who coded themselves as working at a calling reported better life, health, and job satisfaction as well as significantly fewer reported missed days at work. The surprising find-ing was that "satisfaction with life and work may be more dependent on how [employees] see their work than on income or occupational pres-tige."[5]

Wrzesniewski's research further showed that the ability to view one's work as a calling is not dependent on the occupation. A study was conducted across a range of occupations including physicians, nurses, health educators, librarians, supervisors, computer programmers and analysts, administrative assistants, and clerical employees. Across every occupation type, regardless of the occupation's social status, the classification of a job, career, or calling was almost equally distributed (one-third job, one-third career, one-third calling). From administra-tive assistant to physician, about one-third of the people in any occupa-tion viewed their work as a calling.[6]

It's how the work is viewed by the individual, not the social status of the work, that can make it feel like a calling.

People who describe the occupation they are in as a calling describe the work as something they were meant to do. It's easy to imagine the level of fulfillment and height of performance that can be achieved when people are engaged in work they feel they are meant to do. Fortu-nately, doing what you are meant to do doesn't just mean searching for the exact right profession and embarking on a wholesale career change (although that is obviously an option). For most people, in fact, that may not be very practical or necessary. Rather, it's about helping people identify what really matters and calls to them, and then baking in meaning—that is, incorporating rich elements into the existing work and workplace that will help answer the call.

It starts with establishing a clear sense of inner direction, born out of a sense of purpose, desired legacy, and closely held values and beliefs. Our purpose provides direction because it crystallizes why we are working; it is the higher-order end that directs and sustains our energy and effort. Working toward our desired legacy provides direction in that it gives us something specific and tangible to strive to leave behind, which helps bring our purpose to life. Our most closely held values and beliefs serve as a moral compass for our intentions, steering us toward what we feel to be right and setting off alarm bells when we encounter something intuitively wrong.[7] Values and beliefs turn guesses into good decisions. The net result is the establishment and articulation of a clear inner direction that keeps what matters most, what calls to us, at the forefront of our perspective. When we have this kind of meaning in our work, it gives us something to return to after attending to the demands of our jobs that yield less satisfying returns.

With this self-awareness in hand, then, elements of our work can be reframed and reshaped and other elements added in, so that work begins to feel less like something we have to do and more like something we were meant to do. In this manner, when we act to clarify our direction, it is akin to pursuing a calling. Chapters 3 and 4 will discuss specifically how to establish a powerful inner direction and forge work that matters.

DISCOVERY

"Be brave enough to live life creatively. You have to leave the city of your comfort and go into the wilderness of your intuition. You can't get there by bus, only by hard work and risk and by not quite knowing what you're doing. What you'll discover will be wonderful. What you'll discover will be yourself."

—ALAN ALDA[8]

The desire to live up to our fullest potential is one of the most fundamental sources of internal motivation. It's what drives athletes to compete and win at higher and higher levels while they are still able. It's what drives a single mom to hold down two jobs and take classes at night. It propels an accountant to take the stage for the first time on open-mic night at the comedy club. It pushes a pizza delivery person to save up to buy his own franchise.

But when we know deep inside we aren't driving to achieve our fullest potential, it can drive us to distraction. "Is this it?" we wonder to ourselves. It nags at us that we may not be becoming all we were meant to be. While developing an inner direction helps you understand who you are meant to become, discovery opens up the avenues of possibility for you to get there. We all must make choices as we try to live a meaningful life. Choosing a journey of discovery, rejecting the notion of settling, and venturing forth to live up to your fullest potential is as powerful a source of meaning as actually achieving your potential.

In the process of discovery, we can take specific actions to maximize personal learning and growth and help ourselves and others achieve the fullest potential. When striving to reach our maximum ability, we elevate our performance by default.

With all this said, then, why don't we take every action we can in the pursuit of discovery and effort to maximize our potential? What gets in the way?

Is it fear of failure?

Consider a story shared with me by Paul Miller, a former Ringling Bros. and Barnum & Bailey circus clown and owner of Circus Mojo, a company that hires and trains at-risk youths to teach the art of circus as a group activity to forge interconnectedness and strengthen self-esteem. Paul conducted an experiment simultaneously with two groups at his circus teaching facility. One group consisted of about twenty kids from a private school for gifted, high-potential children. The other group of twenty kids all came from a correctional facility, with criminal records and a history of juvenile delinquency. He taught each group circus skills—spinning plates, juggling, and balancing on top of balls. The group of gifted children mastered the skills over twelve hours of instruction across multiple classes.

The kids from the correctional facility mastered the tricks in about twenty minutes.

Why?

No fear.

What did the "delinquent" kids have to be afraid of? They had all been through pretty tough scenarios over and over in their young lives. The gifted children were afraid to fail; they thought they knew everything already and their fear of failure and looking dumb in front of others kept them from learning.

Is there some of this hesitancy and fear of social stigma in all of us?

Or does fear of failure embed deep within us an almost subconscious aversion to risk altogether? A former Yale professor, William Deresiewicz, has argued that you should *not* send your kids to Ivy League schools because the admissions standards have become so extreme that, by definition, those admitted have never experienced failure. Deresiewicz contends that students simply can't experience failure, even temporarily—in fact, the thought of not succeeding terrifies and disorients them and creates a violent aversion to taking risks in the process. "You have no margin for error, so you avoid the possibility that you will ever make an error," he writes. The pressure to succeed that we put on ourselves can manifest itself in our avoidance of challenges, or worse. A large-scale survey conducted among college freshmen (not just those at Yale) found that self-reported emotional well-being is at the lowest level in twenty-five years—a side effect of self-induced pressure to succeed and our intolerance of failure.[9]

When we are not taking on enough challenges, or are not challenged enough in ways that personally energize and stretch us, it means we are passing up the chance to activate the second Marker of Meaning. We derive meaning and heightened output from our work when we are learning something new, taking risks, and growing as individuals.[10] It requires an individual to take responsibility for his or her own learning and growth, but to do so in an intentionally designed work atmosphere that commits to the cause as an imperative. And while it can be meaningful when we are learning what others expect of us in our jobs, it's even more meaningful when what we are learning is congruent with what feeds our interests, speaks to our passions, encourages self-expression, or advances our cause as well.

The problem arises when the challenges thrown at us at work are taxing, but not energizing.

We have all experienced times when we've been given a meaningful amount of new work, perhaps even meaningfully more difficult work. However, it doesn't mean that the work was meaningful to us personally, taught us something new, or was energizing.

As a meaning-making manager, you can better frame the challenges that are necessary but may not be necessarily meaningful to your employee at first glance. You can also help strike a balance between providing challenges of necessity and nobility. Challenges of necessity are intended to move the business forward, with the hope that learning and growth will happen along the way. Challenges of nobility are carefully crafted with each individual in mind, designed to advance the business at hand, first and foremost, but also with the noble cause in mind of tailoring growth to the individual.

Chapter 5 will cover in detail how you can create a meaning-rich personal learning and growth plan. In doing so you can replace a sense of stagnation with an increasing sense of competence and self-esteem—and thus the third Marker of Meaning is invoked as well. When we are working with a heightened sense of competency, conditions are ripe for meaningful achievement. Research shows that when people believe they are developing a sense of felt competence it provides a sense of meaning in their work.[11] Similarly, when people believe they have the ability to make a difference, they have the wherewithal to make meaning.[12]

By enabling a personal learning and growth plan you can serve as a propellant of self-confidence and self-esteem. You can build employees' sense that they are worthy and worthwhile, valued and valuable—a feeling so essential that as humans we go into an almost subconscious survival mode when this sense is in doubt. Social psychologists Roy Baumeister and Edward Jones found that after participants received negative feedback about certain aspects of their personality, they came to view other unrelated aspects of their personality more positively relative to participants who had not received negative feedback.[13]

When self-esteem is threatened, people fight to restore it.

When you act as a supportive, confidence-building manager you can prevent others from having to expend energy to fight that fight.

Continual learning and managerial support in the process feeds our sense of heightened competence and self-esteem, as does a sense of autonomy. When workers have a sense of control over an outcome and feel supported in crafting their own way to achieve that outcome, it is a tremendous source of meaning.[14] Research shows that people have a need to see themselves as capable of exercising free choice and effectively managing their own activities or environments.[15] In fact, a sense of being in control, being able to influence decisions and outcomes, and operating autonomously are vital enough elements that they form the fourth Marker of Meaning.

Easy enough, you say. This is one marker straightforwardly manifested. In the discovery process, granting autonomy and control maximizes meaning. Got it.

Not so fast.

A careful, attentive hand is required as contradictions and misconceptions will arise in the process of facilitating a sense of autonomy and control. Penn State professor Glen Kreiner led a multiuniversity team of researchers that discovered a fascinating paradox. In the quest for meaning, employees will pursue greater control over their own environment (seeking empowerment and autonomy) and yet at the same time seek to *relinquish* control to something greater than themselves (serving a greater purpose) to provide the sense that they are not alone and actually do not need to be in control of everything.[16]

This study hints at the complexity involved in facilitating a sense of empowerment and autonomy, which also has many downsides if done improperly, such as the empowered employees operating without clear direction or not being set up to succeed with their newfound responsibility. For managers looking to ignite meaning in the process of discovery, striking a careful balance is required. You must understand the good and bad that can come with empowerment. You also must balance between the craving for independence and the higher-order needs of a greater purpose within which to serve and a broader community within which to belong. Chapter 6 shows you how to navigate the tricky waters of empowerment and independence. It also illuminates how to involve employees in decision making in a meaning-making and self-potential maximizing fashion.

DEVOTION

Meaning, fulfillment, and corresponding best performance are also born out of devotion. When people feel a fierce sense of loyalty to their work or workplace, it creates a sense that time spent there is of great significance. Read any "Best Places to Work" review or spend time at a few of the workplaces so recognized and you'll begin to sense a pattern of something different at work—a different smell of the place. You can start to sense it with the front desk receptionist in the lobby. You might have friends who work somewhere you suspect you'd have to pry them away from; their sense of devotion is that palpable. Conversely, you might have friends who describe their work environments as corrosive and who say they'd leave at the drop of a hat. What creates the vast chasm of difference?

Choice.

As managers and employees we have a choice to create devotion or devastation in the kind of culture we breed, in the specific daily behaviors we role-model or ashamedly allow to happen, and in *how* we communicate and carry out our mission as leaders (not just *what* the mission is). We just have to know what to choose to do.

Clear themes surfaced from my research in seeking to identify the kind of culture that breeds fierce devotion. And it isn't window dressing, like perks, pay, or power furnishings. Rather, fierce devotion originates in a culture that exudes three elements in particular: caring, authenticity, and teamwork—the underpinnings of the fifth Marker of Meaning.

Perhaps the single most commonsense thread in zealously committed cultures is the presence of genuine caring. When the people you work for, with, and around exude a genuine level of caring for and about each other in a variety of facets, it's easy to imagine work feeling more meaningful and people wanting to take more risk in stretching for personal best performance. Less obvious is what behaviors and actions you, as a manager, can specifically enact that show you to be caring. You first must choose to be a caring manager, then champion the right behaviors to maximize associated meaning.

If caring is one of the most commonsense mechanisms that drives devotion and makes one's work meaningful, then authenticity is one of the most commonly cited. Authentic environments foster a sense of coherence or alignment between one's behavior and perceptions of the true self. The ability to enact or develop the true self helps maintain a sense of meaning and order in one's life.[17]

When a workplace is authentic and allows you to bring your whole self to a work environment that is congruent with your values, you can almost feel your wings unfurling.

The opposite would be a tragedy, as Bronnie Ware can attest.

Bronnie Ware is a palliative nurse from Australia who transformed her life as she spent years tending to the needs of the dying. She recorded themes of regret expressed by those in her care during their last days and applied lessons learned to her own life. She shares the phenomenal clarity of vision that people gain at the end of their lives in her popular blog and book entitled *The Top 5 Regrets of the Dying: A Life Transformed by the Dearly Departed*.

The number-one regret of the dying?

"I wish I'd had the courage to live a life true to myself, not the life others expected of me."[18]

It is our duty as managers, supervisors, employees, and human beings to contribute to an environment in a manner that allows authenticity to blossom.

By the way, I can confirm that "I wish I'd spent just one more day in the office" does not appear on the list of regrets.

Devotion not only arises when people feel genuineness, but when they feel they genuinely belong. Study after study shows that it's not just about how people relate to their work, it's also how they relate to each other. Meaning is greatly enhanced through quality human connection, as is performance: High-performing teams throughout history consistently describe a sense of interconnectedness instrumental to their success. They are devoted to the mission, and each other.

Quite simply, being in a team-oriented environment fosters elevated performance and the formation of meaningful interpersonal relationships. A team of researchers from leading universities conducted a study among faculty at management schools to demonstrate just how much meaning is derived from workplace relationships. The researchers collected stories about why faculty members felt their jobs were meaningful and why they felt a sense of devotion to their jobs. The study revealed that three themes of positive stories consistently emerged, all from the same camp: stories of helping, stories of emotional support, and stories of collegiality. The research further concluded that relationships are not just vehicles to help further career goals, but rather are rich sources of meaning in and of themselves.[19] As a manager, you can facilitate a spirited sense of teamwork that can obviously help nurture such relationships.

But there is something beneath the surface here when it comes to the role that work group membership or being in a team-oriented environment plays in deriving meaning. Oxford social psychologist Henri Tajfel uncovered an extraordinary, counterintuitive finding in a series of studies. Study participants appeared compelled to divide an array of strangers into "us" and "them," even when the basis of categorization was not at all apparent or when the individuals stood to gain nothing personally from so doing. These fascinating studies suggest people possess a tribal impulse that drives them into imagined clans of others seemingly similar to them. The instinctive need for belongingness and being part of a team overwhelmed the basic human need for independence.[20]

As human beings, we have a deeply engrained need to form a social identity.

Social psychologists Michael Hogg and Deborah Terry have found that establishing a clear social identity is critical for reducing a sense of uncertainty; being a part of a harmonious team tells us how to behave and what to expect from the social environment we are in. When threats to this certainty arise, we instinctively fight to protect it. "Black sheep" studies have shown that when a new individual is introduced to a group who brings in behaviors and beliefs different from those of the established group, it creates uncertainty. This uncertainty threatens a clear prototype to which team members have strongly assimilated themselves. Thus, the newcomer is ostracized not because of his or her identity, but because of the threat he or she imposes on the identities of the existing team members. The draw to maintain a clear social identity via membership of a harmonious team is so strong we will quickly create outliers.[21]

The power of this phenomenon is also seen in organizational research done after an acquisition or merger. Many examples of failed mergers exist that attribute the failure to an us versus them dynamic that prevailed as employees wouldn't relinquish their old identities and blend and morph into new ones.[22]

Such is the power of the basic need to have a clear and positive social identity—without it, meaning derived at work goes missing and devotion diminishes. You can make meaning by feeding this primal need through a commitment to fostering a teamwork-oriented environment. The key is actually choosing to foster such an environment and knowing how to do so.

The collection of caring/authentic/teamwork-based elements is the glue in a culture where each individual feels appreciated and cared for, can bring one's whole selves to work, and feels a multilayered sense of belongingness and connectedness. The sum of all these conditions forms the fifth powerful Marker of Meaning. Chapter 7 will show you how to activate this marker by constructing a culture that is centered on caring, authenticity, and teamwork.

While devotion can be intensified with the right underlying cultural framework, it can also be intensified with the right overarching leadership behaviors. As managers and leaders, our actions and words are often on display for the world to see, and they typically resonate beyond our peripheral sense.

Simply put, leaders can create connections or disrupt them with their conduct and communications.

Allowing employees to feel a connection with and confidence in their leadership and the mission (and where they fit within it) is the sixth Marker of Meaning. The reality is that there are certain behavioral musts and specialty skills required from leaders who want to trigger this marker. And it can be tricky science to get the formula right.

For example, it is easy to see how critical it is for a leader to have a clear and compelling vision that everyone wants to be a part of; such a vision makes the organization seem special and drives people's passion to contribute to something so meaningful. However, if that vision is constructed, communicated, and brought to life without a very careful eye toward those who will carry it out, meaning can be lost along the way. The troops have to understand not only where they are going, but why it matters. They want to know that *they truly matter* to help bring it to life.

How you go about carrying out and communicating the vision and mission to the troops is often as important as what the actual vision or mission itself is.

Likewise, it is critical to project confidence in yourself as a leader. A Cornell University–led research team isolated high self-confidence as the leadership variable most correlated with high stock price performance.[23]

However, to truly maximize performance and associated meaning, you must ensure that your self-confidence converts to garnering confidence from the troops. Communicating the right things in the right way at the right times is paramount if you want other people to feel confident in and connected with you and inspired to contribute their best. Anything less will lead to a wake-up call.

Just ask Mark Shapiro, president of the Cleveland Indians baseball team.

Mark was at a friend's wedding. The friend happened to be marrying the daughter of professional football coaching legend Bill Parcells. Shapiro and Parcells were engaged in chitchat at one point early in the festivities and Mark was lamenting the number of player injuries he was dealing with and the aging player roster. Parcells interrupted Mark's diatribe, looked him in the eye, and gave the best advice Mark Shapiro ever got:

"Mark, nobody gives a sh!#."

Parcells repeated the wisdom to Shapiro again at the wedding reception, and a third time in the evening at the urinals.

Shapiro has never forgotten that leaders must lead, that there must be unswerving accountability, and that there are no excuses.

And the troops are watching.

Chapter 8 will highlight the messaging and behavioral musts, leadership traits, and specialty skills needed for you to become a meaning-making leader.

As fast as passionate devotion can be built up, it can be torn down with a few misplaced behaviors (or a poor response to misplaced behaviors). It's a well-known rule of thumb in business that one negative consumer impression can wipe out a hundred positive ones. Corrosive behaviors dangerously lurk beneath the surface of even the most devoted workforce and can quickly bubble up and undermine the meaningfulness felt in one's work. If the behavior perpetuates a breach of trust, it may do irreparable damage to a relationship. Being free from corrosive workplace behaviors is so essential to the derivation or deflation of meaning that it is its own Marker of Meaning—the seventh and final one. Vigilance is required to trigger this marker, as is a trained eye. Chapter 9 will sharpen vision and awareness of the most common caustic behaviors and instruct you on how to cut them off at the pass.

DILIGENCE

All of the Markers of Meaning, when intentionally attended to and wired into a work environment, produce outcomes that truly matter. Chapter 10 helps you craft a specific plan for weaving all the wiring together into a high-powered network of daily meaning creation.

Disengagement, mediocrity, and despair do not stand a chance; the map to meaning creation is now at your disposal.

part two

DIRECTION

CHAPTER 3

The Potency of Purpose

RESEARCHERS HAVE CONFIRMED SOMETHING ABOUT HUMAN behavior that we already know instinctively; it's not our fault, it's just math. When we spend more than half of our waking hours at work, it's bound to happen.

People tend to define themselves, and to be socially defined, by their work.[1]

It's why at social gatherings, when we are meeting others for the first time, talk often turns to inquiries about one's occupation. We're not asking, "So what do you do?" as much as we are asking, "How do I define you, so I can process and categorize you in relation to all the other human beings I know?" We have a natural, even subconscious preoccupation to want to define ourselves and others within a work context.

The problem arises when we don't like the definition.

When our definition of self begins to feel too one-dimensional, lacking in significance, void of direction, or we can just sense we are not living up to our fullest potential, we begin hungering to redefine who we are and what we've become. For many of us, a gnawing sense of unease slowly begins to take form; something isn't quite right in our world, we think. Something's missing. Some may think that they are trapped in their current work-life mode for a variety of reasons. For others, a tragedy might throw their world into a tailspin, causing them to question all the hours they've been putting in at work. Why have they been working so hard? What's the point of it all?

After the events of September 11, 2001, the phenomenon of reexamining the role that work plays in one's life, and how it contributes to the definition of self, was widespread. In the weeks and months after that day, news stories began appearing about the changes people were making in their work lives because of the terrorist attacks. The tragedy had recast how people were thinking about their work and how they were spending their work lives. Many people began reshaping their work or switching careers altogether. Teaching applications skyrocketed around the country, increasing by as much as 50 percent.[2] Tragedy had called into question the role work played in an individual's life, as well as the very definition of self. Many people turned to a higher-order beacon, seeking direction and redefinition of their professional lives. The search for purpose and meaning had suddenly entered the collective conscience.

President Obama, in the wake of the Sandy Hook Elementary School tragedy in Newtown, Connecticut, in December 2012, addressed an entire nation in an attempt to make sense of the madness by asking: "Why are we here? From what do we draw meaning? What is our purpose?" These are the questions of human nature that arise in times of tragedy.

Whether by a gradual awakening or a jolt, the onset of absence of meaning in your work starts to get addressed when the journey of discovering purpose in your work begins. Discovering your purpose and putting it to work *in your work* is how you can take back control. Because the truth is, work does not define you: You define your work, and how it serves your higher-order purpose.

The role that work plays in your life does not have to continue on autopilot, defining more and more of who you are, by default, with each passing year. This course of self-definition by default can be dramatically altered when you stop, reflect, and articulate what your higher-order purpose is and how your work can be recast to serve that end. At that point, the idea of disengagement would be completely out of place.

Unfortunately, the statistics (as laid out in Chapter 1) are stunningly clear: Far too few people in the workplace are even engaged, let alone driven by something as powerful as an articulated purpose.

Imagine the impact you could have on your employees' level of meaning, fulfillment, and performance at work if you could help them achieve such inner clarity. You would be triggering the first Marker of Meaning and allowing purpose-driven work, work that deeply matters, to enter the picture.

Whether you are an already enlightened manager wanting to learn how to help others find their purpose, or a manager needing to first initiate the pursuit for yourself before you help others do the same, there is a common starting point.

It begins with an appreciation for just how powerful purpose can be in helping us to reshape our work lives (and lives in general), how powerful it can be in changing how we view ourselves at work, and how potent it can be in rekindling our fire to bring out the best performance we have inside of us.

THE IMPACT OF PURPOSE

You must first start from a place of understanding exactly what is meant by purpose.

Purpose is the Profound **Why.**

When you are operating with a clear purpose, you understand and accept why you are working so hard and spending so many hours away from loved ones, friends, and family—you can see and sense the higher-order end your efforts feed into. You know why what you do matters. In the absence of a clearly defined purpose, the answers to these "why" questions elude us and our work can come to feel meaningless.

Research clearly supports that work that promotes a sense of purpose nets meaning and fulfillment and correlates with heightened performance.[3] Purpose creates a sense of personal mission to do something worthy. It's what Holocaust survivor and author Viktor Frankl has referred to as "a significant yet to do in life" that gives life meaning. Moreover, Frankl's horrifying experience led him to propose humans simply cannot survive without purpose.[4]

Purpose integrates *who* we are with *what* we do. It inspires us to renew our commitments and stretch even further. Operating with a sense of purpose shapes our work life (and life in general) and gives it intentionality, providing great clarity of direction like an internal compass, to turn to over and over again when we feel we are losing our way or when attending to the day-to-day wears us down. It serves as a vessel for our yearnings and even yields a sense of transcendence, so you feel that you are part of something bigger than yourself.

I've seen it firsthand, when and where I wasn't expecting it. I spent time with the movers and shakers of Silicon Valley, visiting the campus headquarters of Facebook, Google, and Yahoo in Palo Alto, California, and meeting with leadership to find out what made their companies tick. With the Facebook IPO and the stunning stock performance of Google, I expected to find the standard sense of entrepreneurial spirit mixed with a strong undercurrent of an understandable drive for enormous personal wealth, given the size of the business opportunity at hand.

I couldn't have been more wrong.

Sure, I talked with a fair number of likely multimillionaire twentysomethings. However, I don't think a single one of them was ever driven by the prospect of money for the making. Each and every one of the workers I met was representative of the intense, palpable sense of purpose that seemed to hang over their campuses. The employees of these companies truly believe they are changing the world for the better. And they are clearly driven by their inspiring missions to do so.

Facebook's Chief Operating Officer Sheryl Sandberg (and author of *Lean In*) and Sam Lessin, onetime leader of the company's Identity group and brainchild of Facebook's Timeline, both spoke with fervor about their purpose, telling me that it is "a social mission to make the world more open and connected." Lessin spoke of his belief that Facebook will ultimately be about the noblest of causes—making people's lives better. It is in the company's DNA to fundamentally believe that changing how people communicate can change the world—it always has (think telegraph, telephone, computer, Internet, mobile phone). And the belief that the company needs to do so with a tremendous sense of urgency is readily apparent.

In the early evening I walked by Mark Zuckerberg's windowed office, visible right off the main quad (meant to symbolize the desire for an open global community), and saw Zuckerberg himself feverishly pacing around, bouncing a ball off the floor while talking and vigorously interacting with others in his office. The intensity was palpable even from a distance. And that intensity translates right down the line, as I could hear the zeal in the voices and see it in the eyes of everyone I talked to on the Facebook campus. I read it in the handmade posters that employees are encouraged to post around campus with sayings like "People Over Pixels," "Move Fast and Break Things," and "Proceed and Be Bold." Facebook employees are driven, to the core, by their belief that everything they build should facilitate human connection. And to the person, they all said the cause makes them work even harder. Case in point: After Facebook's much vaunted IPO bell-ringing ceremony on the campus, everyone hurriedly went right back to work, with very little fanfare.

It's not about the money; it's about the meaning.

Google leaders spoke of their driving purpose to connect people to the problem-solving magic of search. The only people who get sucked into the glamour of the famed perks (free gourmet cafeterias, sand volleyball courts, dry cleaners, etc.) are visitors. The residents are clearly driven by their belief that seamlessly connecting humans to the world's information will change the world.

It's about the exciting purpose, not the expensive perks.

At Yahoo in 2013, at the time of my interviews, there was a fair amount of turmoil at the top with the changing of the CEO and other top managers. Some employees I met felt Yahoo was drifting a bit. One of the very first moves that Kathy Savitt, chief marketing officer, made was to put into words the *why* of what Yahoo does. Kathy's belief that the why would give shape, guidance, meaning, and accelerated performance to her company speaks volumes to the potency of purpose. Kathy spoke of Yahoo being a "daily habits" company, and that its purpose was "to make the world's daily habits more entertaining and inspiring."

Collectively, much has been written about the glitz and glamour of Silicon Valley and how it houses the most billionaires and millionaires per capita in the United States.[5] However, it is also the most inventive region in the United States, with the city of San Jose alone producing almost as many patents as the entire state of Massachusetts.[6] Behind the inventiveness lies one of the most purpose-driven workforces in the world. Facebook's "hack-a-thons" typify the region's spirit of meaning-fueled imagination. Every few months, Facebook engineers (who lovingly refer to themselves as "hackers") get together for an all-night marathon of writing code. With tents pitched on the lawn and small bands of huge brain cells sequestered, the goal is to think freely, move fast, and convert the spark of an idea (outside of their day-to-day projects) into a working prototype of something that could change the world. The engineers aren't motivated to work through the night until six in the morning to find ways to make the company and themselves more money. They are driven by their aligned sense of purpose to connect more humans and make it easier to share more things.

This kind of intense sense of purpose elevates and stretches human performance and contributes mightily to the profound production of the region. Across employee interviews at some of Silicon Valley's bellwether companies, I clearly saw a drive to deliver on a worthy mission.

The presence of purpose can have a transformative effect on a company. Such power is at your disposal as a leader.

James Moorhead, chief marketing officer at Dish Network, immediately recognized the role purpose could play in a much-needed transformation at his employer, a company that received notoriety as the Worst Place to Work in America two years in a row. Upon arrival, Moorhead rolled up his sleeves and went back to the company's roots to find its purpose. Moorhead told me:

> Dish Network was born out of a desire to serve the underserved—
> those people who lived in areas that cable didn't serve, that
> couldn't get basic services and information. It was founded with

the purpose of giving families access to the world. This story was never told to our 30,000 employees. It inspired our launch of a satellite broadband service; we now give small towns access to high-speed Internet and access to things such as education, for example. We are no longer just about selling paid TV.

Moorhead's passion for purpose has helped step-change business results at Dish Network and nearly double organizational survey scores on related key metrics. The training Moorhead instituted equips employees to bring the newly rearticulated purpose to life and has tripled organizational survey scores on key vectors like "I'm set up to be successful."

Identifying a sense of purpose is no less transformative on an individual level, for you and your employees.

THE PATH TO PURPOSE

So how does one start down the path to purpose? As a leader, you can start by simply role-modeling your company's purpose (and helping to forge one if none exists). This is true regardless of the nature of the industry you work in.

Consider, for example, the story of dunnhumby USA, the world's leading customer science company. Dunnhumby analyzes data and applies insights to create better customer experiences and build loyalty, hardly an obvious hotbed for purpose-rich surroundings. However, the company finds itself annually on several Great Places to Work lists largely because its CEO, Stuart Aitken, is dedicated to role-modeling the company's purpose.

Aitken told me:

Creation of meaning at dunnhumby starts with our purpose: "We do things *for* the customer, not *to* the customer." Accordingly, some of our retail or manufacturing clients don't always like the recommendations we bring. Some of our end-user customers live paycheck to paycheck and we put value in their hands with things like targeted coupon mailings. We start with this clear purpose and put building blocks in place around it to create meaning at work for our employees.

As Aitken walked me around dunnhumby's headquarters, it became obvious he believes in the purpose thoroughly and in role-modeling purpose-driven behaviors for the organization. For instance, Aitken instituted Get Out of Jail Free cards that exonerate an employee from the wrath of a client who wasn't ready to hear the recommendation that resulted in something being done *for* the customer versus *to* the customer. The purpose carries over to how Aitken feels about his entire company of employees; he clearly takes pride in doing things for them, instead of to them.

He showed me the sound-damping open-air work spaces that use fabric to dampen sound and provide privacy while still facilitating a spirit of collaboration and maximizing exposure to the abundant natural light in the building. He pointed out a row of trophies the company received for its impact on the surrounding community. And he showed me the company gym and café with great pleasure. Aitken talked of his love of serving the People Team, a group dedicated to addressing watercooler issues and how much he enjoyed "Coffee with Stuart"—a chance for entry-level employees to connect with their CEO. Aitken stopped in the middle of our tour to profusely apologize to an employee because he had done something *to,* and not *for,* the employee by missing a meeting.

The extent to which the purpose permeated the company was quite evident—from posters on the walls that elaborate on the company's purpose, to the thoughtfulness on display in little touches throughout the headquarters space, to the company's standing in the community, to the "do something for, not to" mindset, which was evident in all the employees I spoke with.

Just as you can embody the company's purpose, you can also help employees discover their own individual purposes (in work and in life).

A six-step process I've developed called the Path to Purpose will guide you through the identification and articulation of your own personal purpose. This process has helped many people (including myself) and has been continually refined over time; it comes from a place of experience, feedback, research, and academic understanding. An important thing to note up front about this process: The speed at which each person moves through these steps varies. For some people it may require a small, concentrated dose of time to work through each of the steps, while others have to think, explore, reflect, adapt, and adjust.

Once you've found purpose, though, it doesn't mean you can't lose it. It's not like riding a bike.

The path never really ends. Over time you'll likely need to retrace some of the steps and repeat some of the in-process activities. Our perspective changes as we get older, we learn new things about ourselves and the world around us, and we have new experiences and uncover new longings. The common denominator that needs to be in place here, though, is commitment to the journey. Once you and/or your employee are committed to the importance of discovering purpose and are convinced of its potency, you are on your way to unleashing the absolute best performance and the best person that lies within.

Let us now proceed with the assumption that you, the manager, will need to walk through the steps of discovering and articulating your own purpose first. Even if you can already clearly articulate your own purpose, the idea here is to learn the steps on the Path to Purpose for yourself so that you are then equipped in turn to help your employees discover and articulate their purpose.

Step 1: Change the Equation

Disappointment and dissatisfaction often result from a gap between an ideal (what we expect, what we hope happens, what we want something to do) and reality (what we get, what actually happens, what something does). This can be expressed as an equation:

Happiness = Reality − Expectations

Now, let's think of the 71 percent of the overall workforce who are disengaged. The reality of what their work delivers is not as great as their expectations, thus creating negative happiness—that is, unhappiness.

To make the equation positive or at least less negative, if employees can't improve their realities, they have to lower their expectations, which is just sad. In fact, research shows that for many of the disengaged, over time a reluctant acceptance creeps in that work can only do so much. They believe that their return on investment from work is low—there's nothing that can be done about it. As disengagement and resignation settles in, expectations of the role work can play in the fulfillment in one's life are lowered in an attempt to at least make the happiness quotient less negative. A vicious cycle can then take hold whereby lower expectations lead to diminished reality, which leads to even lower expectations, and so on.

For your employee (or yourself), the first step needed on the Path to Purpose is to rewrite the happiness equation so it looks like this:

$$\uparrow \text{Happiness} = \uparrow \text{Reality} + \uparrow \text{Expectations}$$

New heights should be set for the happiness quotient. Reality at work should be vastly improved by pursuing purpose and meaning-rich work with vigor. Your expectations should be raised to much higher levels. And don't assume reality and expectations are a zero-sum game. Pride should be taken in how high expectations have been elevated, and when they are met in reality, it should be made an *additive* in the happiness equation. Meeting (not just exceeding) dramatically higher expectations means you've grown. More was expected of your work and more was achieved, which should bring nothing but greater joy and fulfillment to you. This formula promotes a virtuous cycle and replaces the vicious cycle.

Step 2: Change Your Questions

It's time to change the questions you are asking yourself. There's nothing wrong with the usual battery of self-evaluative inquiries: Does my boss think I'm good? How am I doing relative to my peers? When will I get promoted? How much of a raise will I get? What will my next assignment be? Did I come across well in that presentation? All healthy questions, the kind you intersperse in between the cracks of the exhausting amount of hours you are working. The kind of questions you undoubtedly ask yourself multiple times, over and over, throughout your career.

But *why* do you keep asking yourselves these questions?

Consider what happens when a child asks you a question, the same question, repeatedly. Child psychologists will tell you that, besides the obvious fact that they might not understand your answer, children repeat questions because (1) they want a different answer or (2) they want to keep your attention.

Do you ever find yourself playing some of these questions over and over in your head looking for an angle you've missed and trying to forge a different answer; looking for a little more comfort, a little more return on the investment you've made with so many of your waking hours?

Or are you trying to keep your own attention?

As the hours spent at work mount, the interest level can dip, and the meaning of it all can wane. Then your brain conducts a progress report on your aspirations in the form of these questions, looking for a boost of inspiration. However, the truth is, your line of repeated self-questioning in this vein will eventually have the same net effect as a child's repetitive question—you *will* grow weary. And you will draw less and less energy from the answers. After all, you can only work so many hours—be so good in the eyes of so many bosses, get promoted so high or make so much money—before it isn't enough anymore. The gnawing sense that something isn't quite right, that something is missing, slowly begins to kick in. An adverse event sharply brings a sense of self-doubt into your periphery. Then, either with a slow burn or surprising immediacy, your work no longer seems to matter.

Unless you change the questions you are asking yourself.

The questions have to come from a place deeper than a career-related checkup. There has to be a realization that while these types of questions certainly have their place, it's going to take more work to find a purpose in work.

The inner dialogue has to go beyond career inspection to *introspection*. This introspection requires a commitment to carve out time for thoughtful reflection, which can be difficult to do in our harried lives.

University of Southern California psychologist Mary Helen Immordino-Yang says that taking time for this reflection, however, is absolutely essential to our ability to make meaning of the world around us. Taking a respite from things that require outward attention to enable some inward attention is critical for our psychological health and well-being and sense of inner direction.

Immordino-Yang's research indicates that when children are given the time and guidance for reflecting, it enhances motivation, decreases anxiety, increases test performance, and enables better planning. The fast-paced, multiscreen digital environment that children are growing up in could be greatly detracting from their opportunities to inwardly reflect, which could have negative effects on psychological development. It may "rob them of opportunities to advance thinking from 'what happened' or 'how to do this' to 'what does this mean for the world and for the way I live my life.'"[7] It is no different for us adults. We have our own set of multiscreen, fast-paced competing priorities that are keeping us from taking time for introspection. It's keeping us from reflecting on past experiences, analyzing our current environment, uncovering our purpose, and finding deeper meaning at work.

So where to start?

We begin with Michelangelo.

In a letter written in 1549, Michelangelo described the approach he took in creating his breathtaking sculptures. He called it a process of taking away, not adding on (the process used when modeling clay). He'd carve away everything the statue truly wasn't, chiseling away all the debris and all the distractions to free the beauty that had always lain deep inside the confines of the marble rock.[8]

And so it is with us on the Path to Purpose. Over our working lifetime, it is so easy to let the distractions build up, causing us to set the chisel aside. We fall into a course of doing, making, earning, rising, providing, and over time can unintentionally bury deeper and deeper those things that truly give us a sense of fulfillment. But with each introspective question we ask ourselves and answer with clarity, more of the surrounding mass of rock falls away and brings us one step closer to revealing the sculpture we are intended to be. Once you start asking yourself more introspective life questions, you find that what holds meaning for you may well have nothing to do with your long-held beliefs about what constitutes success. Once you start asking these questions, you are on your way to exonerating yourself from one of the greatest self-crimes one can ever commit: leaving purpose buried within. As Oliver Wendell Holmes stated, "Most of us go to our graves with our music still inside us."[9]

Just what are the introspective questions to ask? There's one more interim step before we get there.

Step 3: Put the "Me" in Meaning

This step is brief, but worthy of separate consideration. It is about making yourself a promise, before you begin to reflect on the kinds of questions that get at what will create true happiness and fulfillment in your working life. The answers to such questions cannot be formulated in the light of other people's expectations. You have to resist the temptation to compare yourself to others when answering introspective questions.

This step can be difficult because it requires an unswerving commitment to brutal honesty with yourself and an intense commitment to compare to no one. No matter how difficult your admissions or how uncomfortable they make you, no matter how your answers might cause you to stray from the norm or what is expected, it's important to hold yourself accountable to the truth. What you assign significance to, what truly matters, is highly personal and should not be defined by others' perceptions. There is a "me" in "*me*aning" for a reason. You are the sole scribe of what holds meaning for you. No one else can ascribe meaning on your behalf.

Once you've made this promise to yourself, you're ready to begin the next step.

Step 4: Conduct an Inner Interview

To unlock your purpose is to open your mind to a different set of questions. I've developed a set of powerful questions intended to help uncover your purpose. Each question requires reflection and soul searching and delves into a range of sources for inspiration.

Some questions enable scrutiny of your core essence, getting at the undeniable truths about the blueprint of you that might hint at a purpose you could naturally embrace.

Other questions help you delve into your past, seeking to heighten self-awareness of the times, places, and root causes of happiness throughout your life—all potential clues to what your purpose might be.

Still other questions help you probe what greater good you are drawn to serving, a potentially direct source of purpose.

Finally, some questions force you to consider your aura—the unspoken gestalt others see in you. Seeing the truth behind what others see in you can grant a vision of what your purpose might be as well.

All of these sources give rise to the purpose power questions that follow:

❏ *What are your superpowers?* We're not just talking about what you implicitly know that you're really good at. To be certain, identifying your strong points can point you in the direction of your purpose. However, the question is, what are the strengths that you can use, like a superhero, to do good for others? Our natural talents and developed gifts provide clues for how we might most effectively channel our energy to make the maximum amount of difference on something vitally important to us. It is when we decide that what's vitally important to us is something bigger than ourselves, and that we will employ our strengths to that end, that our powers turn into superpowers. Discovering purpose means fully embracing what you were born to do, but also what you were born to do unto others. So, after reflecting on the former, apply the filter of the latter. It will lengthen your stride on the Path to Purpose.

❏ *What are your values and beliefs?* What matters the most to you? What is not open to compromise? Staying true to what you believe in is a source of great strength and can see you through even the most intense inner conflicts. This same power source can provide clues about what your purpose might be. Our strongest values, beliefs, and priorities often serve as an interim inner credo, a purpose proxy, that we'd be wise to take note of during our journey of discovery. Along the way our values and beliefs give us boundaries to work within. While en route to purpose, you can craft more meaning in your day-to-day work simply by making small adjustments so that your behavior and expectations are all congruent with your values and beliefs.

❏ *What would you do for free?* What are you doing when you lose track of time at work? What do you catch yourself daydreaming about? Committing to something as lofty as purpose feels less daunting when you realize you already are (or want to be) committed to it. The inherent motivation will propel you along the way. Again, it is critical that you are honest with yourself and identify what you actually love doing, not what others might expect you to love doing. To jump-start your thinking, here are nine types of activities we engage in at work. Which are you drawn to?

1. Discovering, innovating, and envisioning

2. Nurturing, growing, developing, and counseling

3. Expressing, performing, storytelling, and acting

4. Designing, planning, building, and making

5. Adventuring, risk taking, and protecting

6. Healing, teaching, and managing

7. Investigating, experimenting, truth seeking

8. Founding, directing, and organizing

9. Guiding and mentoring[10]

❏ *What part of you is not showing up at work?* We are living with purpose when we are bringing our whole selves to the workplace. Try to identify any pieces of you that you have to check at the door; then examine why. This exercise can point to strengths locked within that you are longing to bring out, and may indicate the forces pushing you off the Path to Purpose. You can then formulate a plan to address those forces, attend to your longings, and serve your purpose.

❏ *What have been your happiest moments?* The common elements of your happiest moments, inside and outside of work, can indicate the fundamentals of your purpose. Commit to them.

❏ *What have you learned from career misfires—and triumphs?* Consumer behavioral research indicates that when people are shopping for a specific brand or item in a crowded and confusing category (tooth-paste, for example), they engage in the process of deselection. This is where the mind, in the process of taking in all the information and choices in front of it, automatically takes certain choices out of consideration so it can more easily process what it sees while searching for a desired item. Uncovering purpose can be aided by a similar process of elimination. When we learn to deselect experiences from our past, such as work we simply didn't enjoy, struggled to excel in, or suspect that we weren't meant to do, the way forward to our purpose becomes a little less cluttered. Fewer choices make it easier for the right one to reveal itself.

In this way, the wrong turns we take in our career are some of the most valuable learning experiences we have to draw from. We also glean from our successes clues about a fruitful path toward purpose. During at least some of our successes it is quite likely that we were at our best. And when it comes to analyzing our successes, it is critical to focus on what we did, true?

Well, only half true.

It is as important to reflect on who we were when we were at our best as it is what we did. That is, how did we behave? How did we interact with others? What was our attitude? How did we feel? The totality of this picture could reveal ourselves in our most natural, happy state and hints at the purpose that could help us replicate this state of being at our best.

❑ *What deed needs doing?* What problem needs solving? What does the world need more of that you are well suited to serve? A common misconception here is that a purpose has to be some entirely new need that was previously unmet and unarticulated.

A purpose doesn't need to be unique; it just needs to be you.

Ask yourself, "What is my cause?" What efforts do you donate your time and talents to? Thinking of your purpose at work as a cause is a way to creatively reframe how you spend your time there. One especially passionate group of administrators I met kept piggybanks on their desks marked "Pennies for Purpose." For each small act they conduct during the day that contributes to their cause, they drop one penny through the slot. Little acts interspersed with big acts spell sizable donations to their intended purpose. You, too, can continually seek to make small donations to your cause throughout the workday, while striving to write the occasional oversize check.

❑ *Who would you serve?* Who are the beneficiaries of your servitude? Examining who you find yourself drawn to when it comes to giving of yourself can provide important clues about your potential purpose. Do you particularly enjoy coaching your direct reports? Do you like teaching peers or other professionals? Do you especially like serving the community through your volunteerism? Volunteerism is a great source of meaning and purpose in and of itself, especially for older adults. A study revealed that volunteering helped buoy a greatly diminished sense of purpose among older adults who had experienced the loss of their role identities as wage earners and parents.[11] Beyond volunteerism, do you like being involved in a specific charity?

Now ask yourself why. What is it about these exchanges? What do the recipients receive and return that is so gratifying? Answers to these questions provide clues on the Path to Purpose.

❏ *What would coworkers miss if you weren't there?* A common way for researchers to understand the depth of impact of a variable on its environment is to conduct a deprivation study. Want to learn what impact a Keurig coffee-brewing machine has on a consumer and how it fits into her lifestyle? Take it away from her for a month. Or consider the most famous deprivation study of all time—the story of *It's a Wonderful Life.* Clarence the angel shows George, the central character, what life would have been like if he'd never been born (turns out not so good, and suddenly George realizes the positive impact he's been having all these years). Imagine if you deprived your workplace of you. What would people miss? What do they appreciate most about you? The delightful, unique ingredients that you bring to the workplace stew, and that are most appreciated, can be telltale signs of the positive impact you could aim to accentuate and perpetuate in the name of your purpose.

❏ *What would people say you were meant to do?* What strength or defining characteristic of yours shows up so evidently at work that others would feel compelled to speak about it if asked in your absence? What would others likely tell you that your second profession should be? Thinking of what others would say you were born to do can help give birth to your purpose. Again, that is not to say that you should compare yourself to what others would expect. Rather, others' observations about you are helpful here because they may call to your attention unique skills you know you have that weren't top of mind beforehand.

Step 5: Commit to Something Greater Than Yourself

Having identified your superpowers as part of this process, you next have to commit to producing good for others as part of your purpose. As Muhammad Ali noted, "Service to others is the rent you pay for your room here on earth."[12] This step is so critical it merits its own discussion.

Committing to something greater than yourself means making sacrifices, foregoing taking credit, and setting aside personal gain. It does not mean you have to stop pursuing your personal potential. In their landmark book *Built to Last*, Jim Collins and Jerry Porras wrote of the genius of the "and"—that is, the greatest, highest-performing companies have the ability to deliver seemingly contradictory elements, such as creating wealth for shareholders *and* doing good for the world. They can be values-driven *and* pragmatic or profit-driven.[13] So it is with us.

The greatest level of sustained performance over time comes when we strive to reach our personal fullest potential *and* truly commit to a good greater than ourselves. Pericles, the Greek statesman and patron of the arts, said: "What you leave behind is not what is engraved in stone monuments, but what is woven into the lives of others."

This, from the man who built the Parthenon.[14]

Counterintuitive research findings unearthed in 1990 by noted psychologist Mihaly Csikszentmihalyi have implications for just how powerful the pursuit of the power of *and* can be. Csikszentmihalyi's research detailed the surprising concept of flow: "the state in which people are so involved in an activity that nothing else seems to matter; the experience itself is so enjoyable that people will do it even at great cost, for the sheer sake of doing it." People in a state of flow actually feel a sense of disappointment when they achieve their objective. It is the act of performing a thoroughly enjoyable and meaningful task, not accomplishing the task itself, that drives a deep sense of happiness and fulfillment.[15]

Commitment to the power of *and*, realizing your full potential, and passionately serving others is a task never completed. Find the right purpose and pursue it with conviction and you can live a life filled with many moments of flow.

Step 6: State Your Purpose

Now it's time for the final step in identifying and articulating your purpose—the creation of a purpose statement. It's well known that writing something down increases compliance, so boil down the purpose you have worked hard to identify into a crisp sentence or two. Getting it down precisely will also sharpen your thinking about what you are committing to. Keep your purpose statement front and center constantly. Put it on a card you can keep in your wallet or purse. Make it the home screen on your phone. Recite it in the shower each morning.

The way the purpose statement is written can even elevate the worthiness of the purpose itself and provide further inspiration to pursue it with conviction. The goal is to write a purpose statement inspiring enough to give you goose bumps or make your pulse race. The extra little dose of energy can inspire you to overcome obstacles in the way of your purpose or make behavior changes if needed.

Who can we turn to for help in crafting such a motivating set of words? Who better than the motivational masters of inciting behavior change: the advertising agency.

Leo Burnett is one of the most successful ad agencies in the world and a true master at leveraging the power of language (and visualization) to motivate and affect behavioral change. The company clearly believes in the power of purpose. As Leo Burnett EVP and Strategy Director Wells Davis told me, "A purpose is one of the most human of attributes, as most of us struggle if we feel we are without purpose in life. Brands need a purpose so that they do not wander aimlessly."

Just as important, when a purpose can be crisply articulated, it is a powerful tool for inspiration and guidance. To illustrate this point, consider the work Leo Burnett led for some of its clients, household-name brands looking to develop an inspiring purpose to help guide their brand's activities. The point of sharing this story is not to suggest we all should act like brands trying to sell ourselves, but to show the motivational power of getting your purpose statement *just right*. Look at Table 3-1 and you'll get a sense for how motivating a well-crafted purpose statement can be. Check out the "Before" column for each brand, which depicts an accurate portrayal of the brand's reason for existence, and compare it to the "After" column, which is a rousing expression of the brand's reason for existence—its inspired purpose. If you worked for any of these brands, which statement would inspire you more to bring your absolute best performance to bear?

Table 3-1. *Before and after brand statements.*

BRAND	BEFORE (Accurate Portrayal)	AFTER (Inspired Purpose)
Special K	For calorie-conscious women, a system of balanced food products that help achieve weight loss objectives	Help women achieve a sense of victory
Purina Pro Plan	Balanced nutrition preferred by professional dog trainers and breeders worldwide	Unleash the greatness within every dog
Norton	Software tools to optimize the performance of your PC	Protect digital freedom and fight cybercrime
Invesco	Range of investment products to provide growth and manage risk, sold exclusively through financial intermediaries	Save people from accidental investing
Hallmark	Excelling at ink on paper	Help celebrate life's little moments

No contest, right? In the After column the power of a well-articulated purpose statement is evident; it elevates the brand, and you can just imagine the force of conviction and pride engendered.

The accurate portrayal defines the brand's *worth*; the inspired purpose defines the brand as *worthy*.

You too can evolve your draft purpose statement from an accurate portrayal to one that crackles off the page with motivational energy and potential.

Here's how.

Examine the verb used in each of the inspiring purpose statements in Table 3-1. Help. Unleash. Protect. Save. What is the verb of your purpose statement? Visualizing yourself in the act of delivering the manifestation of your purpose can help crystallize the purpose statement itself. What are you doing? Are you:

* *Creating* a movement of kindness and generosity

* *Unlocking* the potential of every willing person you meet

✳ *Bringing* civility and respect back to the world and to the workplace

✳ *Helping* women to succeed by overinvesting in their success

✳ *Stirring* the disengaged into action and into believing in themselves once again

✳ *Championing* the need for diverse thinking and styles in the workplace

These purpose statements are all real examples, shared with me over the years as an outcome of classes, seminars, or working sessions I've led. Some of them are directed squarely toward work, and some are more broadly about purpose in life, but carefully crafted to be directly applicable to work as well. The verb in each statement was carefully considered to further gel the exact aspirations of the person and the end toward which that person was working.

Another question the experts at Leo Burnett use to unlock interesting verbs is, "What would your purpose liberate you from or free you to do?"

The choice of verb ensures your purpose statement is inspiring, action oriented, and actionable—for you. Again, it is not important that your purpose statement be unique, just that it speak to the unique you. It should just feel right; it should convey that what you've been doing throughout your life adds up to the purpose you have now defined. You share it with friends or loved ones and they say, "Of course—that's you."

PURPOSE POWER-UPS

To supplement the Path to Purpose, here are two techniques for further strengthening a sense of purpose. I've had great success with these techniques: mission fit and job reframing.

Mission Fit

Let us return to a most unlikely source of meaning manufacturing: the Cleveland Indians organization.

In 2007, Mark Shapiro, then general manager of the Cleveland Indians (and a man who would later be portrayed in the film *Moneyball*), defied conventional logic. He stood in the locker room after his Indians had just knocked the mighty New York Yankees out of the playoffs to win the division series, watching the cigars being passed around and the obligatory champagne celebration of spraying and dousing and general merriment. Surely, Shapiro stood among incredibly highly paid athletes (relative to Major League Baseball standards) whose astronomical salaries were now paying the dividends one would expect, right?

But such was not the case.

Money hadn't bought this pinnacle of achievement. Shapiro had eschewed the standard "high pay for high performance" model in baseball. On this night, the entire city of Cleveland watched proudly as its overachieving players enjoyed the fruits of their labor. They toasted Shapiro's shrewd roster signings and eye for underappreciated talent.

But there was something more at work here.

As he stood in the middle of the locker room, surrounded by hosts of cameras and well-wishers, Shapiro looked at all the players in front of him reveling in the moment, while his attention wandered. In the midst of all the chaos, he thought of all the people in the organization who were so instrumental in the players' high level of performance. Behind each of the athletes he saw the physical therapists who had spent countless hours rehabbing the sometimes testy athletes. He found himself thinking of the strength and conditioning coaches who diligently labored day after day with seventeen- to eighteen-year-olds who just might someday be the winning pitcher in Game 7 of the World Series.

He remembered the talent scouts, some of whom had traveled an untold number of miles over and over to watch player after player, often at games with no more than thirty people in attendance. He saw the bench coaches who worked as hard in drills and practices as the players did, day in and day out, pushing them to new levels. He stood there thinking of them all and knew that each and every one of them had performed at the highest levels of their careers too, and were just as responsible for the success the Indians were enjoying as the players themselves.

What drove them all?

Mission fit.

Mark Shapiro made it a point to spend time down and across the far reaches of his organization to ensure that everyone understood the purpose and mission of the Cleveland Indians and how they fit into it. Mark knew he had a resource problem; the bigger market teams had far more resources and revenues than his club ever would. The Indians needed to go about the mission of post season success very differently: by making smart trades, signing free agents, keeping all players healthier than rival teams would, bringing up superior talent from the depths of the farm system, having better analytics, and in general getting the absolute best performance and maximum incremental efficiencies from each and every employee in the organization. It was small-market ball in a big-market sport—not exactly business as usual.

He needed everyone in his organization understanding and appreciating their role in the mission and reframing the standards for success, no matter how seemingly insignificant they perceived their role to be. So Mark personally made sure that each and every scout, trainer, coach, member of the player-development staff, and front-office worker knew how important their work was and how it fit into the mission of the Cleveland Indians. All the way down to the interns who had to break down reams of tape, Mark made sure they understood that their analysis could make a huge difference in giving the Indians an important tactical advantage. And then he left them completely empowered to do their job. As Mark told me, "We've had interns make a huge difference in advancing our mission, because we let them."

He reconnected people in the organization with their work in a new way; he widened his employees' current view of their jobs and helped connect the dots so that they could understand how pivotal they were for accomplishing the mission. He reframed and elevated everyone's work and brought out the worker's best performance in so doing. It was this kind of commitment to creating accountability to the mission and empowering *everyone* in his organization to progress toward the mission that twice earned Shapiro the title of *Sporting News* Executive of the Year and led to the Cleveland Indians being named *Baseball America*'s "Organization of the Year."

Shapiro's story is a prime example of the sense of purpose that a leader can bring to an organization simply by ensuring that each and every person in the organization understands how his or her work specifically ties to the broader mission. A study by BlessingWhite on employee engagement supports Shapiro's discovery. When disengaged employees were asked what would improve their performance, the study found that the number-one item chosen from a list was "greater clarity about what the organization needs me to do—and why." This item was chosen by a factor two times over the next item on the list of options.[16] Simply put, enabling comprehension of mission fit can provide a surge of meaning (and performance).

Job Reframing

When we begin asking ourselves the why questions behind our work, we begin down the Path to Purpose. However, a sense of purpose and deep significance can also come when we ask ourselves *what* the work itself really means, in terms of its end result and impact on others; *who* our work serves; and *how* the work is done. The core of one's work itself may be intrinsically meaningful, given the industry; it's hard to argue the potential for purpose and meaning behind the work a schoolteacher does, for example. Of course, not all work is inherently meaning-rich. However, virtually all work can be imbued with a sense of purpose and meaning. It might just require some reframing, or looking at the work through a different set of lenses.

In many jobs, the significance of what the work itself means (in terms of its end result and impact on others) can get lost in the minutiae of daily routines. Sadly, a sense of purpose and feeling that the work matters can wane. Reconnecting the dots between the work and its impact on the end beneficiary has tremendous power, as University of Pennsylvania psychologist Adam Grant demonstrated in an interesting experiment.

Grant conducted the study among two groups of lifeguards at a community recreation center. Pool lifeguards enter their roles with elevated feelings of significance because they believe they have the potential to save lives—that is their purpose, after all. They soon discover that the opportunity for rescue is rare (beach lifeguards make all the rescues) and their job devolves to a series of highly monotonous tasks—with attention and job satisfaction declining accordingly. The attention deficit syndrome is severe enough that technology is marketed to serve as a "lifeguard's third eye" to sense when a body is motionless in the water and correspondingly send a computerized alert to the lifeguard.

At a staff meeting, each group of lifeguards was given a separate set of four stories to read over a fifteen-minute period. The first group read news stories about lifeguards who rescued drowning swimmers. The second group of lifeguards read stories that highlighted how the skills they learned in lifeguarding would go on to benefit them personally in life.

The results?

A full six months after the first group had read stories for just fifteen minutes about other lifesaving lifeguards, they were still volunteering three more hours per week and getting much higher ratings from supervisors on helping behaviors than before. The group who had read stories of self-benefit had no change to their behavior.

Grant maintains that there is often a disconnect between how employees perceive the task significance of their work and the actual impact of that work on the end beneficiary. People want to know their work matters, and if the connection is lost, it's not surprising that a felt sense of purpose in the work sneaks out the escape hatch, too. He further maintains that managers can do three things to reframe and help employees make the connection:

1. Introduce employees to their end-customers. (Medtronics medical equipment engineers have watched formerly paralyzed

patients cartwheel across a stage at an annual meeting—
thanks to their work.)

2. Gather stories for your employees. (Volvo engineers get to read
   stories about their beneficiaries from the Volvo Saved My Life
   club.)

3. Encourage employees to share their own stories and open up
   discussion on the purpose and significance behind their
   work.[17]

The cues employees receive about the importance of their tasks are
something that can be part of your meaning-making reframing plan.
Professor Jane Dutton at the University of Michigan showed that
cleaners at progressive hospitals don't see themselves as janitors but
instead as part of a team that delivers health and well-being to their
guests.[18] Or consider the fable of the stonemasons. As the story goes, a
traveler came across three stonemasons breaking granite in a field. The
traveler asked the first one what he was doing. "Why, I'm breaking this
granite," came the reply. The same question to the second mason
produced the response: "I'm building a wall." The third stonemason
had an altogether different answer: "Well, I'm building this beautiful
cathedral."

How many employees are made to feel like they are breaking granite versus building a cathedral? The purpose we find in our work soars
as high as the definition we assign to the work itself. Changing the
view of *what* the end result of the work really means has more impact
on the pride, sense of purpose, and height of performance than one
can imagine.

Another way work is reframed is by considering *who* the work
serves. Let us consider some of the more difficult jobs to glean purpose
and meaning from. Workers in so-called dirty jobs with stigmas
attached to them must inherently suffer from low occupational self-
esteem and pride and a dearth of meaning, right?

That would be a misconception, as shown in a study by Arizona
State's Blake Ashforth and Glen Kreiner. Ashforth and Kreiner conducted a study on work-related self-esteem and pride among groups of

people working in what society would consider disgusting, degrading, or stigmatized jobs (e.g., sanitation workers, bill collectors, miners, janitors, shoe shiners).

They were surprised with what they found.

While these workers were well aware of the stigma attached to their jobs, they maintained a highly positive sense of self in the workplace. For example, two-thirds of a prison guard sample agreed/strongly agreed with the statement "People are more sympathetic to inmates than to correctional officers," yet when asked to describe their job to others, half of them described themselves as "very or somewhat proud." How do they do it? To be sure, they create occupational subcultures that give them perceived protection and a place to commiserate and forge bonds of brotherhood. More important, they reframe their work by considering who they serve (the public they protect). Public defenders view themselves as serving and protecting "the constitutional rights of all citizens and their right to a fair trial," not as lawyers helping rapists and drug dealers beat the system. Or funeral directors state they are helping relatives and friends deal with grief, rather than processing dead bodies and profiting from their work. Hospital orderlies remark that medical procedures could not be performed if they didn't transport patients around the hospital.[19]

The point is, even those in what might be viewed as meaning-challenged jobs have found a way to reframe their work to help derive a positive sense of self and lay a groundwork for derivation of meaning and purpose. Reconsidering who they really serve has served as a powerful source of inspiration—an applicable lesson.

Reconsidering *how* you go about your job is the final way you can help reframe and reconstruct a new work worldview for your employees. We've all stopped and smiled when we've observed a fast-food worker or traffic cop attacking their job with an outward zeal, smile, or even a song. How they go about the matter of their work can make their work matter.

I was at a children's museum once with my daughter and struck up an unlikely conversation about purpose with a maintenance worker. He was attacking his job with gusto; in between his more "menial" duties he was offering helpful directions, addressing every passerby with a smile and hearty hello or a well-whistled tune, and joyfully and jokingly on the prowl to find things to fix. He told me he felt it was his calling to take a stigmatized job like a maintenance worker and do it to the best of his ability, like no one had ever done it before. In this way he would inspire all the other workers who had jobs of seemingly lower social status. He showed me a card he kept in his wallet that was inscribed, "My purpose on this planet is to make the 'menial' magical." He had reframed his job, and completely reframed my expectations.

You can do the same for yourself and those around you.

CHAPTER 4

The Lighthouse of Legacy

IN THE WORLD OF MARKETING, WHEN A CONSUMER WON'T TRY A given brand, the search begins for "barriers to trial." It might be a bad experience with the brand, too high a price, a desired attribute that's missing, or many other possible reasons.

When it comes to leaving a legacy at work, there are two barriers to trial. The first is the fact that some people simply don't think about leaving a legacy at work. They think of legacies solely as a pursuit for one's life outside of work. The second is the belief that legacies at work are only for those with great stature and resources at their disposal. Boldly restructuring a company to position it for growth? Now that's a legacy. Developing a game-changing vision for a faltering division and implementing that vision to yield a business turnaround? Certainly impressive footprints in the cement. "But what could *I* do that would qualify as a legacy?" many of us think. "I'm just a _____."

If you've run up against either barrier, this chapter will change your mind and show you how to get past it because, respectfully, both barriers grossly underestimate the power of anyone, in any position, to make a real difference at work. The scale might be different, but the relative impact doesn't have to be. I've seen it time and again as I've worked legacy plans with people across all levels of an organization.

65

65

Powerful legacies are planned and achieved by the upper ranks of management, to be sure. But some of the most compelling personal missions and personal transformations come from lower-level employees striving to leave legacies behind. Here are some actual examples of legacy statements from such employees:

> "I will transform our 1-800 line into an insight and trial generator."

> "I'll create a better expense processing system—we're spending twice the time we should be!"

> "I will make this project twice the size with half the resources."

> "I will turn this team's internal navel-gazing into an external obsession."

> "I will give my boss one-third of her time back through smart calendar/time management."

In each case, the result achieved was no less impactful in its environment than what a CEO might put in place. And the pride, energy, and elevated performance unleashed en route was transformational for the individual.

Anyone, at any level, can leave a legacy behind.

And striving to do so, like when you are working toward a purpose, means you've activated the powerful first Marker of Meaning: doing work that matters.

THE DIFFERENCE BETWEEN LEGACY AND PURPOSE

Legacy and purpose are mutually supportive yet unique in the role they play in unlocking meaning, the best performance, and a sense of deep fulfillment. If purpose is the Profound Why (Why are you working and why are you here on this planet?), then:

Legacy is the Profound **What.**

It is about the specific, lasting impact you make. What are you working on, of meaning, to tangibly leave behind? What will outlast you that helped make your purpose concrete? If purpose gives you a sense of direction, like the North Star, legacy guides your activity and course taken along the way, like a lighthouse that steers you and keeps you off the rocks.

Identifying your purpose (Chapter 3) can serve as the initial step in identifying and articulating the legacy you want to leave behind. Then you can turn next to enacting a specific plan to determine what your legacy will be—what will survive of you that helps bring substance to your higher-order purpose.

THE PIVOTAL MOMENT

"You can't do anything about the length of your life, but you can do something about its width and depth."

—EVAN ESAR[1]

Esar, a popular American author and humorist, had it exactly right: We may have a limited number of moments, but we can expand the impact of each moment considerably. Each moment can also be the pivot for all those to come after. So while a legacy seems very far off, the best way to ensure it is to start now—at work and in life. Think of it as meaning's 401(k).

And the investment in this case is your directed effort and intentionality to leave the legacy you want.

Let me tell you the amazing story of a man named Alfred.

Alfred was a very wealthy Swedish chemist who made a fortune off his inventions of dynamite and other explosives that came to be used as brutal weapons in warfare. In 1889, his brother Ludwig was killed, ironically, in one of Alfred's dynamite factories. A local newspaper writer got his facts mixed up and, believing that it was Alfred who had died, not Ludwig, wrote an obituary about the wrong man. Alfred woke up one morning and stared at the newspaper with a truly astonishing realization—he was about to read his own obituary. And so he did.

Only he didn't like what he read.

The paper called him "The Merchant of Death," referring to the fortune he made off of the misfortune of those who were victimized by the weapons he had created. Alfred realized with painful clarity the legacy he was careening toward, and it exasperated him.

He knew he had reached a pivotal moment in his life. He had to change the course of what he'd be remembered for.

From that point forward he dedicated his time and considerable fortune to honor and advance acts that benefited, not obliterated, humanity.

And thus, Alfred *Nobel* established the Nobel Peace Prize.[2]

Alfred had the rarest of opportunities, the chance to see what he'd actually be remembered for while still living. He had a chance to rewrite how his life story would read, and he seized it.[3]

Hold that thought.

Now let me tell you about a man named Gregg Snouffer. Gregg is an outstanding high school teacher in Columbus, Ohio. But that's not why I'm sharing his story. Gregg also happens to be the head coach of the U.S. Boomerang Team.

Who knew such a team even existed? But indeed it does. There are five core events in a competition that tests the thrower's ability to throw and catch a boomerang for distance, accuracy, speed, and so forth. The World Cup of Boomerang is played every two years; the United States won the World Cup under Snouffer's tutelage in Rome in 2010. The global sport depends heavily on a few U.S. sponsors to fund travel around the globe, and in fact most boomerangers play the "strange little sport," as Gregg describes it, for that exact opportunity—to travel and see the world. In the summer after the U.S. World Cup victory, Gregg faced a challenge he didn't see coming—a challenge none of his peer coaches in U.S. sports had ever faced.

Very few people showed up to try out for the team.

They were otherwise engaged in a variety of other sports or distracted by video games, mobile devices, and whatever else young people tend to get involved in. The pipeline was drying up. Without interest from the next generation of players, serious trouble loomed.

The sport of competitive boomerang faced extinction—on Gregg Snouffer's watch.

Now, granted, it wasn't as if a beloved species of animal was about to be wiped from the planet, but that's not the point. Gregg saw a path ahead that he couldn't accept. He was simply not going to let it be his legacy; he would not let the sport of boomerang fade into the sunset while he was at the helm.

He knew he had to reach active, sport-minded youth, the target audience for creating the next generation of players. So he did something radical for any sport and for any coach: He took the promotion of the entire sport into his own hands. He nicknamed the best throwers on his team the "Rad Revolution" and made them the poster boys of the sport. He engaged the team in a series of training camps in touristy areas so that the stars could build skills and camaraderie and raise awareness of the sport. After an intense period of targeted training, Snouffer had drummed up interest in the sport once again, restocking the feeder system and effectively saving the sport of boomerang.

In his pivotal moment, Gregg, like Alfred Nobel, changed the path that lay before him and positively altered the outcome for generations to come.

I share these two stories because I'd like to propose that each of you is currently at a pivotal moment.

You just might not know it.

Is your business languishing in the face of an unprecedented level of challenge from a particularly fierce competitor? Are you being forced to continually do more with less, pushing you beyond the brink of effectiveness? Are costs creeping up, forcing you to cut corners on materials that go into your product and triggering an unease that the frog has begun to boil? Perhaps your friends and family are quietly suffering because you are simply working too much or are not present enough when you are with them.

Whatever the circumstance you find yourself in, you may well be in a pivotal moment; you just have to recognize it and decide it's time to take control of the legacy you leave.

It may well be time to change course and envision a greater legacy, then get after it with such energy that it recasts the challenges you are facing and expands the impact of your future moments in meaningful ways.

Here's how.

THE FIVE FOOTPRINTS OF LEGACY

It starts with an awareness campaign. If you are made aware of how as human beings we tend to leave legacies behind at work and in life, how we leave footprints behind, then you can begin working to make such imprints, even if just a few, each and every day. At the same time you can enjoy the daily doses of meaning that go along with those efforts. Through many years of research and experience I can tell you there are five footprints to be found. Let's look at each of these footprints, or ways in which you can leave a legacy behind.

Enduring Results

The most obvious way we leave a legacy is through enduring results. These are major accomplishments that you envision, invest in, drive to realization, and ultimately leave behind that you can look back at five to ten years from now with tremendous pride and say, "I did that. That simply would not have happened if it were not for me." (By the way, the number-one interview question I ask when looking to bring someone new into my organization is in the same spirit.) By major accomplishments I don't just mean you restructured your company. Major can certainly be impressive results, but it also can simply mean real things you did that touched real lives of real people. We'll come back to the topic of leaving a legacy through enduring results a bit later in this chapter.

Transfer of Knowledge

When we take the time to share what we have learned with others, it is one of the most direct ways we make a lasting impact. At work, we can make an investment in coaching others and in sharing information beyond what's merely required for employees to do their jobs. This transfer of knowledge is accomplished most effectively when you understand how the person you are coaching receives, processes, and retains new information and learning. Not everyone learns in the same fashion—that's why it's called a transfer of knowledge, not a transfusion of knowledge. (Chapter 5 covers learning and personal growth in depth.)

Passing on Values and Life Lessons

If you've followed the Path to Purpose process from Chapter 3, you have a clear idea of what your values and beliefs are. The little things (and big things) we do each and every day are all opportunities to reinforce who we are and what values we hold. The values you live and the life lessons you pass on to others have a surprisingly lasting effect.

Just consider the stories of Jonathan Edwards and Max Jukes.

Two famous studies involving these men illustrate the depth and breadth of impact that a person's values and actions in life can have on family members. Edwards and Jukes were central figures in families that had wildly different reputations and composition. Each man had several hundred descendants/in-laws who were analyzed as part of the studies.

Jonathan Edwards was a pastor and an author with the highest of morals. He was a hardworking, well-educated, disciplined man.

Max Jukes was cut from a different cloth. He was an uneducated, undisciplined, vulgar, and criminal-minded man who was averse to steady, hard work.

An analysis of how a host of family members of both men fared

over time (shown in Table 4-1) reveals a contrast that couldn't be more
stunningly polar opposite.

Table 4-1. *A lesson in the values we live
(the Jukes-Edwards study)*.[4]

Descendants/in-laws of Jonathan Edwards	Descendants/in-laws of Max Jukes
• Over 100 lawyers	• 130 criminals
• 30 judges	• 60 thieves
• 13 college presidents	• 7 murderers
• 60 authors	• 310 who died paupers
• 100 clergymen, missionaries, and professors	• 20 tradesmen, of which 10 learned a trade in a state prison
• 80 elected to public office, including 3 mayors, 3 governors, 3 senators, several members of Congress, and one vice president (Aaron Burr)	• 50 women who led "lives of notorious debauchery"
• 75 army or navy officers	• 300 who died early in life

Source: A. E. Winship, *Jukes-Edwards, A Study in Education and Heredity,* 1900 (Reprint
Apr. 14, 2005, www.gutenberg.org).

The values we choose to live and exemplify and the lessons we pass
on have a reverberating impact on those we interact with every day—
more than we can imagine. Said another way, the little daily impressions we make, inspired by or in spite of our values, make a huge
permanent impression. And distractions abound each and every day
that can keep us from enacting even our most closely held values.
Goethe warned us of this danger when he wrote, "Things that matter
most must never be at the mercy of things that matter least."[5]

It is a worthwhile exercise to crystallize the exact values and life lessons that matter most to you and that you'd most like to pass on. To further inspire you to do so, consider the following.

Imagine that you were asked to write a letter to college students in which you gave insight about what you know now that you wish you'd known when you were their age.

One winter, Professor David Gould from the University of Iowa did just that. Searching among University of Iowa alumni over the age of fifty, he solicited responses to the question, "What do you know now that you wish you would have known when you were in your twenties?" He intended to collect the letters and share them with his students.

The depth, breadth, and impact of the responses was so overwhelming, he turned the exercise into a national initiative called the Legacy Letters Project.[6] Authors responded in a variety of forms, including fifteen-page letters, poetry, short stories, and bullet point lists. Some people offered personal contact information for follow-up or even offered to speak to students in class.

Gould expected the positive response from the appreciative students. He was caught off guard at how cathartic and meaningful the exercise was for the authors.[7]

The power flows two ways when you take the time to be very intentional about passing on your values and life lessons. It is meaningful for you as you convert your wisdom into a living legacy, and equally meaningful for the recipient, who is all the richer for having received the knowledge. What may seem like simple, hard-learned truths to you might be profound advice for another.

Each of the legacy letters that Gould collected bears this out, ringing of a "profoundness and a poetry refined by the wisdom of experience." Each letter proved wrong what Gould calls "the biggest fallacy—that we think we don't have wisdom to pass on."[8]

One particularly poignant letter extolled the virtue of maintaining balance in your life. The author wrote that the exercise of writing the legacy letter "makes you think about if anything you have ever done in your life is worth taking up the time it takes to tell it." The author also sagely advised, "Your health—mental, physical, and emotional—is predicated on balance. How much you give for how much you get. A barter system if you will, where you pay with your life." The author further expounded, "In the end, it is not how much success you have, but how much of your humanity you were able to keep in attaining that success." The letter closes with the thought that "your choices and the control you have is the only gift you get to keep."

Timeless, legacy-worthy advice passed on for others to learn from. From whom, though—a high-powered business executive, a senator, a legendary football coach?

No—how about a supermodel.

Carol Alt, dubbed by the press as "the first supermodel," a woman *Playboy* magazine once called the Most Beautiful Woman in the World, a bestselling author, award-winning actress, skincare entrepreneur, and charitable tour de force, wrote her legacy letter with a sense of humility, wistfulness, and urgency to impart lessons learned. She wondered if any of the students to whom she wrote would even know that she graced the cover of over 700 magazines ("Can they name even one for certain?") or that she was the first model to do posters and calendars. She lamented spending so much of her time on the road and focused on her career, instead of having invested in more lasting pursuits. She wrote of missing birthdays with her family, even her own. She lamented modeling in Paris when her sister had her child, shooting a movie in Miami when her grandmother died, calling on Easter to say hello from the Champs-Élysées, "a long-distance voice on the wire." She cautioned with great resonance, "Have you jeopardized your soul for one small step ahead in business?"[9]

Such is the wisdom of someone who has learned much, the hard way, in life's journey, successful though she may be by other people's measure.

Such is the wisdom you have to pass along, encasing it in a lasting legacy as you go, if you are intentional.

It is vital to act on this insight, and act now, because one's legacy will only become even more resoundingly important as time passes. A landmark study sponsored by Allianz Insurance found that leaving a legacy (an emotional inheritance) was far more important to people than leaving a financial inheritance—in fact, *seven times* more important. Of baby boomers and their parents, 77 percent rated "values and life lessons" as the most important legacy they could receive or leave, while only 10 percent of boomers said that a financial inheritance was most important.[10]

It's meaning, not money, that matters.

Relationships and Lives Serviced

When we invest in relationships and friendships in our professional lives (and life in general), it produces meaningful connections. And yet for many of us, hectic days, spent doing tasks bereft of meaning, prevent us from making even little investments in friendships ripe with meaning. In fact, a Gallup poll showed that just 30 percent of employees have a best friend at work. Tom Rath, author of *Vital Friends*, indicates that "those who do are seven times more likely to be engaged at work."[11] Investing in relationships is critical not only for sustaining maximum performance, but also for sustaining maximum connectivity to something that really matters.

And time won't wait for us to figure this out, either.

According to Bronnie Ware, who documented the top five regrets of the dying, the number-four greatest regret of those in the last days of their life is: "I wish I had stayed in touch with my friends."[12]

Putting energy into relationships that matter to us will matter in the end.

Relatedly, to touch lives is to live in service of others. A simple truth is that people don't remember us for what we do for ourselves; they remember us for what we do for them. Want to leave a legacy behind? Live in service of others with a desire to touch the lives of as many people as you can in your time on this planet. There is a great proverb that says: "If you are intentional about living a meaningful life and leaving a legacy behind, you never really die. Instead, you break into a thousand pieces, each of which stays alive within the people whose lives you've touched along the way."[13]

How remarkably, wonderfully true.

Stories Told About You

The last way we tend to leave a legacy behind is through the stories told about us. What are the big, sweeping tales that characterize who you are? What will be said about the little impressions you left behind and the small gestures you made along the way?

What will be said about you from the heart, when no one is looking?

How did you live your life?

And make no mistake, stories will be told about you. Author Charles de Lint spoke truly when he said, "We're all made of stories. When they finally put us underground, the stories are what will go on."[14] That's the case in life, and it's no different at work. Ever find yourself discussing your boss over the dinner table? If you are a boss, what do you think your people are discussing over dinner from time to time?

It's worthwhile to check in on how the "stories of you" read. You might be surprised by what you learn. Enroll people you trust to tell you the truth about the anecdotes of your travails. One senior leader I know uses reverse mentors, people lower in the organization structure who have agreed to be open and honest with him about the net impressions he is leaving behind. Once you are armed with the gift of true perception, then match up the stories you hear with how you'd like them to go. Hire yourself as an editor of the eternal and rewrite as necessary.

Each step you take in creating your legacy will also bring your purpose to fruition because *what* you leave behind is a direct manifestation of *why* you work and *why* you're here in the first place.

One of the most obvious purposes for us to be at work, and one of the most fertile grounds for leaving a meaningful legacy, is to deliver enduring results—results that matter. Let us now expand on this pursuit. What follows is a process to inspire and produce business results that are truly legacy-worthy.

THE FIVE-STEP FOOTPATH TO
LEGACY-WORTHY RESULTS

Step 1: Appreciate the Power of Legacy and Commit

Work feeds your family. Leaving a legacy at work *feeds your soul.*[15]

Yet when I ask people, "What will your legacy be?" they usually respond with a blank stare then say, "Hmm? What a good question. I haven't really thought about that yet." As the discussion continues, however, passion and emotion escalate as people begin to articulate what's important to them and what they think they'd like to be remembered for. Invariably, you can hear it in their voice. You can feel the emotion in the words. You just have to get the conversation started.

The journey toward identifying what you want your legacy to be starts, oddly enough, with a stop. When you can stop for a moment, break out of the temporal day-to-day, and begin deeply considering the permanent tomorrow you want to work toward, it's liberating.

Forever has a way of providing perspective and prioritization.

That's the power of working toward a legacy.

How did I come to this realization? Was it something I learned from a wise mentor, a former professor, an expert in the field of human psychology?

No. It was the captain of a fishing boat.

I was on a deep-sea fishing excursion, right about the time I also happened to be in the middle of a reevaluation of my work life. The first inklings of the power that pursuit of a legacy could have had just begun to enter my consciousness. On this particular day, my mind was nowhere near this lofty topic, but much more grounded in the simple thought of relaxing and catching a nice, big fish. I had been on several such excursions before and enjoyed them each and every time.

For whatever reason, however, this time was different. A bout of seasickness struck me. Most people who have experienced seasickness will tell you that it is one of the most unpleasant feelings humanly imaginable; curling up in a ball and quietly dying seems a viable alternative in that moment. While I sat bent over and fifty shades of green, the charter captain approached me and gave me the simplest advice. He said, "Stop staring at the roiling seas all around you; pay it no mind. Instead, pick a point on the distant horizon and focus with all of your might on that point. In time, your stomach will settle as the near-in turmoil loses its impact."

I remember it striking me immediately at the time—queasiness and all.

It occurred to me then that that's the power of keeping your desired legacy out on the horizon in front of you and locking in on it. It gives you a great sense of inner calm and focus, something of great significance and personal meaning to hone in on and steer toward while cutting through the turbulent ups and downs of the day-to-day. It energizes you tremendously as you keep revving the engine in an attempt to actually reach that horizon and feed the instinctive drive for progression. Said another way, the best level of performance simply cannot surface and be sustained without a higher-order calling to steer toward over time.

Mehmet Yuksek, CEO of Perfetti Van Melle USA, a global candy company with brands such as Mentos and Airheads, draws on the power of legacy to help him through tougher days and to keep him steering toward the horizon. Yuksek told me:

> The CEO job is one that can be very lonely at times. I continually revert back to my purpose, passion, and desired legacy as my compass and source of energy renewal. My desired legacy is clear—to bring the most value I have in me to the people and the business. When I remind myself of this, it gives me strength and drives me forward once again toward success.

Yuksek serves as an example that when you are able to articulate your legacy, you can continually use it as a guide to stay on course.

And that's not all. The truth is, truly amazing things happen once you've committed to the idea of legacy.

If you invest in legacy, yes, you will become more successful. That's good—that's part of the pursuit, of course. But the real power comes from the fact that you'll move from being merely successful to being significant.[16]

I mean significant for the impact of what you'll put in place, significant for the results you'll ultimately leave behind, significant in the lives of other human beings. We all have a "start date" and "end date" in our lives, and within each of the roles we take on at work, actually. Leaving a legacy is about filling the time in between those two big dates with significance.

When you consider your legacy, you must consider what happens "in between." Stopping to reflect on what chapters must be written in the story of your life before "The End" and committing to writing the narrative you want is powerful beyond description. It changes everything. Once you take a few steps, you will want to take more.

Committing to legacy work can take us from merely being, to becoming.

The events on a cold morning in Washington, D.C., January 2007, underscore this point.

On this morning, a street musician in a baseball cap wandered into the D.C. metro subway station in hopes of making a few bucks. He quietly began playing his violin after dropping a few starter dollar bills in his open violin case. He played for about forty-five minutes, during which time about 1,100 people passed through the station during morning rush hour on their way to work. It took about three minutes before anyone seemed to notice him. Thirty seconds after that, he got his first donation of a dollar, dropped into his hat by a hurried passerby. The six-minute mark finally brought someone who stopped and listened, even if it was only for a minute.

And so it went during the time he was playing, with very few people even acknowledging his existence, let alone stopping to listen. On several occasions, a child, hand in hand with his parent, tried to stop and listen, resisting the gravity of Mom's pull. Each time the stronger of the two won and the child was quickly hurried along. When all was said and done, the man collected just over thirty dollars in tips. He unceremoniously picked up his violin case, put the money in his pocket, adjusted his cap, and headed out into the cold D.C. morning, leaving the metro as quietly as he entered it.

Just another street musician plying his craft among the masses.

Except he wasn't.

The "street musician" was actually Joshua Bell, one of the greatest musicians in the world. He had just finished playing (with gusto) some of the most intricate pieces of music ever composed, on a violin valued at over $3.5 million. Three days before he had played for a full house at Boston Symphony Hall, with tickets priced at a hundred dollars per seat.

To be precise, by the way, he collected $32.17. Some people had even thrown pennies in the open violin case as they dashed by.

This all transpired thanks to an experiment conducted by the *Washington Post*. It was intended to be an experiment in context, perception, and priorities as well as what *Post* writer Gene Weingarten called "an unblinking assessment of public taste—in a banal setting at an inconvenient time, would beauty transcend?"[17]

Apparently not.

We're not evil. We're just mind-numbingly busy and preoccupied. So many of us would have whisked by Joshua Bell that January morning in the metro, latte in one hand, cell phone in the other, on our way to do what we do.

But here's the thing.

All around us, every single day at work, *people are playing their instruments for us*. They are practicing the art of not just being, but becoming—something greater, something that's just below the surface waiting to come out, something that stretches what they thought they could do. They might not be playing an instrument valued in the millions of dollars, but they are playing on their own tools of the trade, in their own way.

Do we notice?

Do we see and hear them playing their instruments for us?

When you are in the throes of pursuing a legacy, it changes the way you view the world. Your eyes widen; you suddenly are more in tune with others playing their own beautiful instruments all around you because you are trying to do the same. You are stretching, pushing, playing your own instrument to the best of your abilities. You now have vision you didn't have before. You see others trying to do the same in their own way. And you want to help them. And you want them to help you in your pursuits. What a wonderful virtuous cycle.

That's the power of legacy.

When we don't notice others stretching, becoming, it violates a core human need to be accepted and appreciated. A core need that we all have, even Joshua Bell. Interestingly enough, Bell was nervous before he started playing that morning in the metro. Why? Bell explained after the experiment was over: "When you play for ticket holders you are already validated. I have no sense that I need to be accepted. I'm already accepted. Here, there was this thought: What if they don't like me? What if they resent my presence?" Similarly, Bell described the "awkward moments" of his incognito performance, when he finished playing a piece he'd just poured his heart into and no one applauded. He had to nervously just pick up where he left off and keep going.[18]

In the workplace, our lack of attentiveness can be taken as a lack of attachment. When you pursue a legacy, though, you elevate, and you notice others elevating. Attentiveness and appreciation become secondhand when you watch firsthand the magnitude of impact that pursuing a legacy can have.

The stories of Joshua Bell and of the fishing boat captain, and others like them, can be shared with an organization to spark an appreciation of and a commitment to invest in legacy-worthy work. It is important to engage the heart and mind when it comes to enrolling others in the power of legacy. The pursuit of a legacy is as emotional as it is cerebral. The permanence granted by legacy in the face of mortality ignites the heart, while the power of possibility and what could be sets the mind ablaze.

Step 2: Color-Code Your Work Plan

Having shed light on the power that legacy holds, we can now look at the work we do each and every day in a new light. The next step on the footpath is actually a step back—to view the work plan through a new perspective and one of three color-coded classifications:

Red—Low-value/low-growth work that we need to stop doing. This is work to delegate, either because we do not uniquely add value to the work or someone else may be better suited to do it. Or if it is truly low-value work that no one should be doing, this is work to eliminate.

Green—High-value/high-growth work we need to keep doing. This is work that is important to the business and a source of personal growth for the individual.

Gold—Legacy-worthy work that will help *define* the lasting impact we leave behind. Investment in this work will pay dividends professionally, personally, and permanently.

Let's first focus on the red and green classifications of work. Any work plan should be constructed to maximize personal growth and maximize contributions and performance for the business unit one presides in. To do so, we first embrace a mathematical incongruity.

Addition by subtraction.

The idea is to focus the work plan to maximize high-value/high-growth output (color-coded green) while minimizing the low-value work (color-coded red) that has a way of creeping into our work lives over time. This requires taking a fresh look at how you are spending your time at work and making a commitment to delegate or eliminate code-red work. Simply put, removing this work will make a difference in your ability to make a difference.

Next, evaluate your current work plan with the following criteria in mind, identifying high-value/high-growth work that:[19]

* Meets the needs of the business (i.e., is aligned with key strategies, goals, and priorities)

* Has clear deliverables that are measurable and time-bound

* Has unique impact and allows the person to receive credit for results

* Builds core skills for the person

* Stretches the person (i.e., allows one's capabilities to be fully utilized)

* Leverages natural strengths and allows the individual to work on opportunities

* Reflects tenure

* Stands up to peers

* Sets up the person for achieving the next level

* Serves the PIE model (i.e., allows a chance to show Performance, enhance Image, and get Exposure)

Holding your work plan to these standards will maximize the green on your work plan.

Now it's time to go for the gold.

Gold refers to the Profound What—your legacy. Ask yourself the following three questions about your work plan:

1. What projects are truly legacy-worthy?
2. Do I need to craft a legacy-worthy project from the ground up?
3. Can I make current elements of my work plan more inspiring and/or transformational?

Not everything you work on has to be a direct feed into your desired legacy; that's not the point nor is it practical. Rather, the thought here is to ensure that there is *defining* work for you to put your heart into. Furthermore, planning legacy work is not a disguised effort to get you to do more work, but to make the work you do more inspiring. Making deposits into the meaningful side of the work ledger gives you energy and more than offsets the energy withdrawals that more pedestrian work can extract. More overall vitality at work means more vigorous performance. And progress on the higher-reaching legacy work, by default, means improved results and a permanent impact.

The key is to view your work plan with a critical eye and remove the red, feed the green, and establish the gold.

However, as it turns out, being hard on your work is hard work. The next step will help.

Step 3: Choose Your Investments for Enacting a Legacy

After reflecting on your work plan, you might feel that you do not have any gold nuggets. You might need help identifying or crafting the gold work and recasting your work plan to be legacy-worthy. To start, you must determine where to invest your time and energy in order to forge a legacy. The following questions are designed to uncover which investments are the most worthy to you. I've found them to be extremely powerful in practice. One manager I worked with on identifying his desired legacy actually tattooed one of the questions on the underside of his forearm to serve as a permanent (literally) source of inspiration!

❑ *If I knew I wouldn't fail, what would I try?* Imagine the courage you'd have if you knew you wouldn't fail. Imagine what bold goals you would set to achieve. Rear Admiral Grace Murray Hopper once said, "A ship in port is safe, but that's not what ships are built for."[20]

We aren't built for port, either.

Think about something audacious you've daydreamed of accomplishing at work. Is a fear of failure holding you back? This self-reflective question is about stretching limits, testing boundaries, and challenging assumptions. As we broaden our horizons, we narrow our inhibitions. And we expand our chances of discovering legacy-worthy pursuits.

❑ *What would take the business to another level?* Write your work plan in two columns: What will grow the business, and what will take it to another level? Don't confuse the two because they produce very different mindsets and very different activities. Imagine the types of projects you'd take on if you set out to absolutely explode the business. Imagine the answer to the question, "What will truly be different, truly have step-changed, because of me?"

❏ *What missing accomplishment would cause me to label my life's work incomplete?* What task would gnaw at you most if you simply ran out of time to complete it? What are you so passionate about advancing that it pains you to be unable to give it attention and activity? In this case, absence does not make the heart grow fonder—it causes it to palpitate.

Identifying what you feel a deep-seated need to get to can help uncover the legacy you want to leave behind. And it's important to remember that legacy work is about feeding your soul, not just your family. So it has to be uniquely about you. Honesty is essential here. Don't just think about what you are supposed to be passionate about. Don't use the word *should*. Meaning at work is derived from what makes your soul sing, not just singing along in the choir of expectations. Again, there is a "me" in meaning for a reason.

❏ *What can only I lead?* Think of the superpowers you identified in Chapter 3. Having your natural gifts fuel your efforts can spur very tangible outcomes and vastly accelerate your progress on the footpath to legacy-worthy results.

❏ *What would I be proud to tell others I lead?* The ego isn't all bad. In fact, it can be used as a definitive source of good when it comes to identifying and propelling one along the footpath to legacy. When we take pride in something, it's because of the difficulty of the journey in getting to the end result, as well as the net impact of the end result itself. Imagining what accomplishments would produce moments of hard-earned pride is a powerful way to identify legacy-worthy work.

❏ *What would competitors be afraid I was doing?* Oftentimes the best performance comes from inspired imagining of how to ensure a competitor isn't as successful. So be it—that's business. It's fair game to leave a mark by leaving a mark of a different kind on competition.

❏ *What could I put in place that will outlast me?* Sometimes it helps just thinking about the passage of time. Some things we accomplish are meant for the moment and are more transactional in nature. Those are often the things that absorb a tremendous amount of our time. Step back and think what would stand the test of time and still be in place long after we are gone from our work role or even from this planet. These are the things that are especially worthy of investment and willful enablers of a legacy. These are the things that will have made time spent in your current job, or on this earth, most worthy. As developmental psychologist Erik Erikson once said, "I am what survives of me."[21]

❏ *Who do I admire for the difference they've made, and what about them could I emulate?* Leaders who inspire us do so because of who they are, what they've done, and how they do it. We can take cues from the net impression and depth of the impact they leave behind. Their actions are a source of inspiration from which we can pattern our own steps along the footpath to legacy-worthy results.

Step 4: Write Your Legacy Statement and Align Your Legacy Projects

After reflecting on each of the questions in step 3, your desired legacy will start to come into focus. To put a point on it, it helps to capture the desired legacy in a written legacy statement, similar to a purpose statement. The examples shared at the beginning of this chapter are all actual legacy statements written by impassioned employees. Let me now offer a few more examples from a range of management levels for further inspiration. Note the mixture: Some of the statements are based on specific business results, some are focused on impacting others, and some touch on both (all viable options):

"I will transform our supply chain into a competitive advantage."

"I will be remembered for always seeing the best in others, not the worst."

"I will sell-in distribution for a critical product line where all others have failed."

"I will be remembered as psychopathically optimistic."

"I will change the category by inventing a . . ."

"I'll be known as the initiative and individual igniter; every idea gets bigger, every person gets better."

As you are writing your legacy statement, it is helpful to cross-reference it with your purpose statement (if you indeed have created one from the work outlined in Chapter 3). Remember, your legacy statement can absolutely live on its own, independent of or in place of a purpose statement. It is particularly powerful, however, when you can devise legacy and purpose statements that work in support of one another. For example, here are my purpose and legacy statements:

My Purpose: Unleash in others an even better, happier version of themselves.

My Legacy: I will inspire actions, thoughts, and feelings that fulfill—every day.

When I was able to articulate *why* I worked—to unleash in others an even better, happier version of themselves—I began to hunger for *what* I could specifically put in place that would outlast me and that would help activate my purpose. Engaging in this sequence of thinking, along with following all the steps on the footpath to legacy-worthy results, helped me uncover my desired legacy and my legacy statement. It began to clearly surface in the form of a wish to infuse inspiration into others to take actions, have thoughts, and experience feelings that all fostered a sense of fulfillment. Thus, a desired legacy was born that was interwoven with my purpose.

At this point, having identified what you want your legacy to be and what the work to support it will look like, it's time to put a support structure in place. That means working with your manager to align projects that will most directly feed your desired legacy. You must set mutually acceptable goals, both long term and interim, and then hold them sacred. Goals are particularly powerful when it comes to the pursuit of legacy. They help sharpen the definition of success for each step along the footpath to legacy-worthy results. Goals also help maintain focus and encourage elevated performance over a sustained period of time, which is especially critical when you are pursuing something as long term as the establishment of a legacy.

A study done by Yale University showed just how powerful goal setting can be for driving sustained performance over time. Yale surveyed its graduating class in 1953 and discovered that only 3 percent of graduates had written goals. Twenty years later, the same class was surveyed and an astonishing fact was revealed. The 3 percent of students who had formulated goals had accumulated a net worth greater than the other 97 percent of students combined.[22]

With goals set, you must next get set up to win by securing the resources needed for your legacy work and by making choices on your work plan as identified by the color-coding exercise (step 2). You can even go public with your legacy work if desired by enrolling a legacy partner who may be a friend or coworker. Then two people, both working toward their legacies, can commit to infusing accountability and inspiration into the other's efforts over time.

Finally, you can also track your progress and get help busting barriers along the way. And barriers will arise. As Mike Tyson once said, "Everyone has a plan, until they get punched in the face."[23] Be ready to bob and weave.

Step 5: Be Attentive to "Others-Focused" Vehicles for Legacy-Worthy Results

Meaningfully impacting others can be as important as any lasting business accomplishment. Being mindful of and attentive to key others whom you'd like to impact, and being intentional about how to impact them, is the final step on the Footpath to legacy-worthy results. We can draw from some of the five footprints of legacy as a source of assistance here:

❏ A *transfer of knowledge* can also be thought of as an enduring result that can take place with direct reports, coworkers, mentees, or those newly entering a job you are leaving, for example. Who is your student body for transference of your knowledge? Overinvest to make a legacy-worthy impact.

❏ Passing on *values and life lessons* can be thought of as an enduring result that requires willing recipients who find you a credible source of learning and inspiration. Who might be your target audience for wisdom that lasts a lifetime?

❏ *Relationships* we build and *lives we touch* can also be thought of as perhaps the most deep-seated, enduring accomplishments we can muster—and both involve an intentional selection and nurturing of intended targets. Think of three relationships you want to invest in and strengthen. Think of whose lives you'd most like to touch.

These others that you will deeply impact are no longer people you merely interact with frequently. They are now vehicles through which you can leave a lasting result; thus, they are an integral part of your legacy plan. Be mindful to elevate their status in your work life (and life in general). This will in turn elevate the likelihood of realizing the full legacy you want to leave behind.

Journalist Sydney J. Harris once said, "Happiness is a direction, not a place."[24] When you embark on the journey to leave a legacy behind and to live with clear purpose, rest assured you'll be bringing along a calming sense of inner direction as a travel guide. When you do so, inspired performance, deep meaning, fulfillment, and, yes, happiness will most certainly be travel companions as well.

part three

DISCOVERY

CHAPTER 5

Learning and
Personal Growth

THINK BACK TO A TIME IN YOUR CAREER WHEN YOU WERE THE MOST frustrated and unfulfilled. There's a good chance it was during a period when you weren't challenged, learning, and growing, when you thought, "Am I wasting my time here?"

Scholars have long held that when we see ourselves learning and growing, it creates an increased sense of competence, which in turn provides a great sense of meaning in one's work.[1] Indeed, challenging people in ways that personally energize and maximize individual learning and growth is the second Marker of Meaning, and it leads to the third Marker of Meaning—working with a heightened sense of competency and self-esteem.

Each new learning and growth experience provides perspective that leads us to recast and retell our life's narrative a bit differently. With each new discovery, we unveil a little more of our fullest potential, the pursuit of which is satisfying and the outcome of which is gratifying beyond measure. Some of the most meaning-rich organizations understand and embrace the impact this force can have on the individual and on the individual's performance.

Learning organizations believe an environment that facilitates high-performance learning is not only essential for personal fulfill-

93

ment, but is absolutely critical to compete. Ray Stata, former chairman of Analog Devices and a pioneer in creating learning organizations, said: "The rate at which individuals and organizations learn may become the only sustainable competitive advantage."[2] A study by the Brookings Institution revealed that 60 percent of an organization's competitive advantage is derived from internal advancements in knowledge, innovation, and learning.[3]

Steve Shifman, CEO of Michelman (a fast-growing specialty chemicals company), told me the need for a learning organization is an absolute essential: "Otherwise the bell curve shifts to the right with today's rate of change and our knowledge base slides toward the average middle." In other words, what we know today that provides competitive advantage will be cost-of-entry knowledge tomorrow, and without continual learning, we'll soon fall behind. In fact, studies show that knowledge gained in college becomes obsolete in two to five years for many disciplines.[4] Shifman further described learning and growth as the centerpiece of his company's operating model and believes it is the very definition of facilitating a sense of meaning from one's work: "Meaning at work comes from knowing I am providing for learning and growing experiences that people just wouldn't have if it were not for their time at Michelman. It can shape their lives."

Former Disney chairman and retired Procter & Gamble CEO John Pepper calls growth one of his North Stars (one of three, actually, the others being service and leadership). The eleventh floor in P&G's central headquarters houses the company's top officers, in half the space it once did. The other half of the floor has been turned into meeting rooms for all and renamed "The John Pepper Learning Center." Another former P&G CEO, Ed Artzt, once addressed a graduating Harvard class with the exhortation to "pick a company that wants to invest in your growth."

So when it comes to maximizing meaning from one's work, continual learning and growth isn't just important, it's imperative. However, fostering a true learning and growth environment is trickier than you'd think.

There are forces working against you that you are not even aware of. Imagine you were given the choice to root for one of two superstar athletes. One athlete is the striving underdog who busted her tail to learn, excel, and get to where she is. The other athlete is blessed with innate abilities—speed and height, for instance—that brought the player success more easily. We'd root for the former—we all love a hardworking underdog, right?

Harvard psychology professors Mahzarin Banaji and Chia-Jung Tsay would beg to differ, and back it up with a fascinating experiment they conducted among a group of professional musicians.

In preparation for the experiment, the professors wrote two descriptive profiles for two equally accomplished pianists. The profiles were very similar, except for nuanced descriptions of how the pianists achieved their musical accomplishments. One described the pianist as having achieved status through hard work and an intense practice routine, while the other cited an abundance of natural ability as the reason.

The musicians participating in the study first read the "hardworking" pianist's profile and listened to a short accompanying audio clip, then were asked to rate the pianist's perceived talent and likelihood of success, and their own willingness to hire the pianist. The participants then repeated the process with the second profile and audio clip from the "naturally talented" pianist and were once again asked to rate the pianist on the same variables.

The study participants were then asked to rate the extent to which they valued innate ability versus hard work and effortful training as contributors to musical achievement. What were the results?

The musicians clearly indicated they valued hard work and intense training over natural ability, as evidenced by how they scored the importance of each of these factors. And yet they clearly rated the pianist described as having an abundance of natural ability as more talented, more likely to succeed, and more hirable than the hard worker.

By the way, both profiles and recordings were sourced from the same woman, pianist Gwhyneth Chen.

The experiment indicates our hidden human bias to speak to the virtues of hard work, and yet revere natural talent. In the study, the musicians' underlying biases to favor the natural very clearly won out. Banaji and Tsay confirmed this underlying bias in other fields as well, such as entrepreneurship, sports, and dance. This naturalness bias is an unwarranted one, however, as research consistently shows it is the striving behavior that yields the greatest performance.[5]

At work this bias subconsciously leads us to unwarranted evaluations on ability and potential, and causes us to undermine the value of what a learning environment could bring out in any striver.

It's just easier to let the naturals rise to the top and set the pace, instead of investing to bring the strivers along. And it's all too easy to let our biases assign star status to the naturals while the strivers have to, well, strive to achieve such status. Such unfair assessments can lead to unnecessary discouragement and, again, short-circuit the realization of a striver's full potential.

Understanding these biases helps you better see the investment it takes to enable maximum learning and achievement for all your employees. And the payoff is more than worth the effort, as management professors Gretchen Spreitzer from the University of Michigan and Christine Porath from Georgetown University have discovered. When high-energy strivers, or "thrivers" in their parlance, were equipped with a plethora of learning opportunities, they demonstrated 16 percent better overall performance (as reported by their managers) and 125 percent less burnout (self-reported) than their peers. They were 32 percent more committed to the organization and 46 percent more satisfied with their jobs. They also missed much less work and reported significantly fewer doctor visits. In fact, those who had a lot of vitality (i.e., were high energy) but had a low amount of learning opportunities were 54 percent worse when it came to health than those who were both high energy and had a high amount of learning opportunities. Differences in other performance measures were similarly exaggerated when looking at employees with high energy only versus those with both high energy and a high amount of learning opportunities combined.[6]

The astounding impact that creation of a learning environment can have isn't limited to game-changing statistics, either. It can be game changing for one's station in life as well.

I introduced you to Paul Miller, owner of Circus Mojo and supporter/hirer of at-risk youths, in Chapter 2. Some of Paul's employees come from correctional facilities and define their status by their criminal records. He tries to change their definition of status by turning them on to the power of learning. And the desire for the change of status—from the guy who stole more cars to the one who has learned to juggle more balls, spin plates quicker, or walk on a balancing ball longer—drives their performance. One young employee of Paul's desperately wanted to perform in front of the general public, eager to show off some newly learned acting chops as a gingerbread man in a bit with Santa. He forgot his bus card and ran *four miles* to get to the facility to perform. And he performed great. He was that hungry to change his status. Says Miller, "New behaviors and a voracious appetite for learning emerge from these kids because they want to change their status so badly."

Whether it's feeding and fueling the striver, or simply helping to elevate someone else's perceived station at work (or in life), you have the power to create meaning and generate sustained elevated performance by facilitating learning and growth.

Armed with an understanding of the impact of such efforts, you can now work to achieve what Stanford University psychologist Carol Dweck calls a "growth mindset" toward intelligence (the belief that through learning and growth we can increase intelligence over time) versus a "fixed mindset" (as humans we have a certain amount of intelligence and that's that).[7]

The different mindsets lead to a very different set of behaviors. Those with a fixed mindset who believe their intelligence level is set can miss opportunities to learn because they do not want to look dumb or have to admit deficiencies when trying something that stretches them. The fixed mindset crowd believes that you are smart only if you succeed without effort. This point of view is very counterproductive to learning because it is the very effort we put into the process of learning that increases our knowledge base and ultimately intelligence. In fact, Dweck's research indicates that the teacher or coach should place emphasis on the challenge and reserve praise primarily for the effort and process of learning, not as much for the actual successful outcome or the intelligence called on to achieve the outcome.[8] These are the underpinnings of a growth mindset.

And a growth mindset is the playground of the meaning-making manager.

THE LEARNING AND GROWTH ENVIRONMENT

When you operate within a growth mindset, the enhancement of your employee's intelligence and ability is limited only by the number of connections to learning and growth opportunities that you as a manager/coach can create. Here are seven ways to build such connections, thus yielding an environment maximally conducive to learning and growth.

Method 1: Learn About Learning

I still remember an animated discussion I had with a high school math teacher about the relevance of geometry. "Learning is learning," he said finally. And while he may have been right regarding his expertise (geometry is geometry, after all), he wasn't entirely right about that statement.

Learning, in fact, isn't learning—not all learning is created equal, at least not when it comes to how adults learn. Facilitating a meaning-rich learning environment in the workplace starts with being mindful of what adult learning experts, such as Malcolm Knowles, the grandfather of adult learning, have taught us about how adults actually learn. This list of adult learning principles is inspired by such teachings and by my personal experience. These principles will help you transport quality learning from the classroom to the conference room.[9]

❏ *Draw on their experience and what they know.* When adults receive new information, they will compare and contrast that new information with what they already know; this process of reconciliation helps them to learn. By comparison, children aren't gifted with a set of life experiences to draw from, and so they are much more likely to accept what they are being told. You can help the adult worker draw similarities and differences between old and new experiences to help cement learning. Likewise, you can provide context on the bigger picture to further facilitate the connection to what the adult learner already knows. Furthermore, recognizing and respecting the value of the adult learner's prior experiences encourages the person to further add to his or her experience and knowledge bank.

❏ *Attend to attention spans.* The adult mind can maintain rapt attention for about twenty minutes at a time. But that oft-heard estimate has dramatically changed for the worse. In today's world of saturated social media, endless quick-burst stimuli on the Internet, and the proliferation of technology, average attention spans have plummeted to *about eight seconds.*[10] For any classroom or training program that relies on a speaker/audience approach, it is important to be mindful of this reality to maximize the power of the learning experience. Breaking up lectures or presentations with visuals, videos, audio, discussions, and stories can substantially expand the mind's ability to stay engaged. Great content and context can further expand attention spans.

❏ *Provide opportunities for immediate practice.* Adults want to put what they've learned to use, fast. Creating opportunities for adults to practice and play with what they've learned at work makes the learning stick and is more likely to create a feeling of increased competence.

❏ *Make clear the personal relevance/value of the learning opportunity.* While children will most often simply accept the process of being taught, adults need to understand why they are engaged in a learning process and how it benefits them. This is especially true in a work environment, where many priorities press at the would-be learning adult each and every day. And while children tend to be focused on more extrinsic factors for learning, such as being able to do as their friends do or to avoid being reprimanded by parents, for adults, the motivation to learn is intrinsic—whether it's to learn new skills to make them more promotion-worthy, to learn how to solve a specific problem, to feed a desire for an increased sense of competency and self-esteem, or to nurture a love for continual learning in and of itself. The point of learning for adults has to be clear and linked to their self-interests.

❏ *Ensure self-directed learning.* Adults want to be more self-directed and active in the learning process, whereas children are more passive in the process and dependent on an adult instructor to feed them the requisite learning. Adults don't need or want a lot of supervision. For you, this means facilitating the learning process versus overdoing oversight of the process. Micromanaging the learning experience will drain the potential fulfillment and meaning to be derived.

❏ *Leverage mistakes as learning opportunities.* Adults view learning from mistakes as one of the most valuable, potent learning experiences of all. That is, as long as the fear of being reprimanded for those mistakes is completely absent from the potential learning environment.

❏ *Take into account different learning styles.* Adult learning expert David Kolb spells out the four different learning styles that adults exhibit. Matching up each learning style with the individual can help better facilitate the learning process and increase the odds that meaning-rich learning and growth will follow.

1. *Divergers* learn by watching and looking at things from differing perspectives. They gather information, listen to others, and use imagination to solve problems and learn. They perform better in brainstorming with others.

2. *Accommodators* are hands-on, relying on intuition rather than logic. They learn from concrete experience and will rely on others for knowledge instead of spending time in their own analysis. They are likely to prefer working in groups.

3. *Assimilators* prefer a logical, precise approach to learning that includes explanations and logical theories. They prefer reading, reflecting, and having a chance to think through concepts on their own.

4. *Convergers* first think through a problem and then use their learning to resolve that problem. They are more likely to experiment with new ideas and then to apply what is learned to practical situations.[11]

Identifying the right style can be as easy as asking people how they like to learn (while explaining each style) or experimenting with each. And for those who prefer a more social learning experience, organize accordingly. A good part of the meaning derived from the learning process can come from the interaction and sense of shared journey one feels when engaged in the learning process with others.

Method 2: Be Conducive to Learning

The extent to which people in your shop are learning and growing in their role doesn't solely depend on the subject matter. It also depends on the extent to which you believe the subject matters.

You have a choice whether to prioritize your employee's growth. Managers who make employee growth a priority exhibit certain behaviors, and their actions help create a safe, thoughtful learning environment. Here's what you can do to foster a sense of discovery for your employees:

* Have patience and empathy for the learning process (and tolerance for mistakes).

* Have a "not yet" mindset versus a "you failed" mindset.[12]

* Put emphasis on assets, not deficits.

* Listen for understanding, not for convincing others.

* Focus on being interested, not interesting (to encourage learning and sharing).

* Enable ownership of ideas (don't do too much for them).

✳ Use data to go from "I think" to "I know." But don't let "I know" get in the way of "I think."

✳ Talk openly about the importance of learning. Role-model the priority you give to learning.

✳ Encourage "the sky's the limit" thinking, not limited thinking.

✳ Commend (not condemn) the person who brings conflicting information.

✳ Don't rewrite history, remember it. Then use realizations to move forward.

✳ Change "we've tried that before, sorry" to "let's try that again, smartly."

✳ Show a genuine interest in each individual's unique learning journey.

✳ Take the time to teach in teachable moments.

Method 3: Practice Managerial Metamorphosis

We've always heard that managers need to be predictable and consistent. In fact, we'll discuss this more in Chapter 9. But when it comes to maximizing learning and growth for others, this isn't always true.

To enable learning, you have to metamorphose into a number of different roles at various times as a manager to help promote a learning environment:

❏ *The Role Model.* By default, your employees are continually learning when they are carefully watching someone they wish to emulate. As managers, we live in a fishbowl where we are constantly teaching, whether we intend to or not. Role-model the right behaviors, actions, and skill sets and you will be creating a constant, compelling curriculum for the eager employee/student.

❏ *The Mirror.* Some of the richest learning at our disposal is what we learn about ourselves. We cannot hide from what we see in the mirror. You can help your employees to clearly see their own reflection and gain insight from it. When you serve as a mirror for your employees, you help them see themselves and/or the situation at hand for what it truly is. Taking the time to gently place the mirror in front of the employee can bring powerful truths to the surface. The employee will then be staring new learning and real growth right in the face.

❏ *The Challenger.* When you disrupt complacency or routines with provocative questions and calls to action, or when you challenge thinking and the status quo, learning and growth are sure to emerge. Consider the science of exercising. Health experts will tell you that it's important to get regular exercise, but not to follow the same exercise routine. Why? Over time when the same exercise routine is repeated, the body gradually becomes more efficient; it is able to do the same amount of work it did previously with less energy. This results in less fat breakdown, fewer calories burned, and ultimately more and more discouragement. Your exercise routine needs change and tension to break the cycle of adaptation and stagnation.[13] So it is with the status quo at work—we fall into routines where we have gotten efficient, but deficient in stretching our brain muscle. You can introduce healthy tension as a manager and get the employees' minds working against new challenges, taking new risks, and experimenting more, thus reinvigorating growth.

❏ *The Sounding Board.* Ever hear someone say, "I'm thinking out loud here."? Well, oftentimes, that means he or she is learning out loud, too. When we have someone to bounce thoughts off of, it helps us to adjust, sharpen, confirm, or reconsider our thinking. When you are serving as a sounding-board partner, offering up even the slightest twist on thinking can introduce a new frame of reference, expand the mind, and lead to new learning and growth.

❏ *The Field Operative.* It is all too easy for an organization to get buried in the day-to-day and look up at some point realizing it has drifted and is out of touch with the external environment. You can play the role of a CIA-like field operative by continually scanning your environment and seeking to increase awareness of what is happening externally. This activity can include facilitating intervals of competitive analysis, getting out in stores to see how the organization's product or a competitor's product is showing up, or reconnecting with end-users to see how their point of view is evolving. Helping the organization stay in touch generates externally focused learning and is a powerful additive for an increased sense of felt competence.

❏ *The Advocate.* When you advocate for someone, you increase (or even directly impact) that person's likelihood of securing new, exciting roles. These new roles mean new learning experiences for the recipient. Don't underestimate the impact you can have on someone's learning, growth, and fulfillment by helping that person get these new experiences and stretching opportunities.

❏ *The Dispatcher.* We learn and grow in the face of challenges. As managers, one of our central roles is to place those challenges in the hands of our people. You can provide work plans and disseminate information as a manager, of course, but you can also dispatch stretching projects and tasks that expand your people's capacity, minds, and potential.

❏ *The Sponsor.* A sponsor serves as a barrier-busting, resource-acquiring, influential force for a project team. Sponsors are usually connected to resources and decision makers and can use their influence to help teams accomplish their goals. Teams learn and grow from achieving such success. They also learn from barriers and failures encountered along the way—learning that the sponsor can ensure doesn't go by the wayside, by taking time to digest such things with the team. In addition, a sponsor's wise counsel throughout a project's life cycle serves as a real-time learning aid. Be a sponsor for a project team, or assign one.

❏ *The Teacher.* Perhaps the most obvious way to facilitate a learning and growth environment is to personally take on the role of teacher when appropriate. The key is to carve out the time it takes to teach others. Even taking time to "describe the view from the window seat" will be appreciated and will offer your employees a good way to get perspective they would otherwise not get. Taking time to build your students' or employees' confidence and self-esteem along the way is equally vital.

❏ *The Designer.* The spirit of this chapter is captured in this role. The idea is that you can intentionally design learning and growth experiences for your employees that will contribute to meaning, fulfillment, and sustained elevated performance.

Method 4: Reimagine Their Jobs

In Chapter 3 we learned about job reframing, or how to view the work one is doing through a variety of lenses to increase its sense of significance. Job reimagining starts with the mind-opening thought that all work is malleable and encourages adjustment of the actual work one is doing to better imbue it with meaning.

Imagine if you thought of work as a set of building blocks you can reconfigure to maximize engagement, learning, growth, and value brought to the workplace. Imagine if your workplace and manager were flexible enough to empower you to adjust your tasks, relationships, and responsibilities (while still serving the requirements of your core role with excellence, of course). Professor Jane Dutton from the University of Michigan calls this practice "job crafting," an expression I've scaled up to "job reimagining," to be more indicative of the creativity required by the manager and employee involved.[14]

Sounds good on paper, but it wouldn't happen in the real-world workplace, right? A job is what the description says it is, and that's what people do.

Not necessarily.

Turns out your people aren't doing the work you think they are.

Job reimagining happens when people feel their need for enrichment is not being met in their job as currently designed. In fact, a study showed this phenomenon is happening everywhere, just largely unnoticed.[15]

Given the runaway rate of disengagement in the workplace, it shouldn't be too difficult to believe that workers make adjustments on the fly in an attempt to survive and find some level of joy and meaning in their work. Even if they are fully engaged in their work, it's human nature for people to try to do more of what they love and more of what challenges them at work.

An administrator takes on projects behind the scenes to learn something new and expand her skill sets. A data analyst who happens to be savvy in social media teaches an informal class to marketers to help them create better marketing plans and push her own level of mastery on the subject. A lab chemist learns how a profit-and-loss statement works from an energetic finance manager. Research shows hairdressers almost instinctively seek to derive more meaning from the task of cutting hair by weaving in conversation, making the effort to learn more about their clients and disclosing personal information to create stronger, more enriching relationships.[16]

No one asked these people to take on these tasks. It's not in their job description. But they do it to keep themselves challenged and to grow. They do it to add more value to the workplace and feel more valued themselves. Psychological meaningfulness of work results when people feel worthwhile and valuable at work.[17]

In addition, with job reimagining, new relationships are created; the nature of existing relationships is altered; and exciting, challenging new tasks are integrated into the workday.

Employees will go as far as to find ways to build their calling into their work. Remember, work can generally be grouped into one of three classifications: a job (means to an end), a career (path to achievement and prestige), or a calling (work infused with personal meaning and intrinsically enjoyable). A study on callings revealed that "people do not simply accept the tasks and roles that managers outline for them. Instead, they actively shape their lives at work to incorporate or emphasize aspects of their unanswered callings."[18]

Indeed, I've come across many such stories where someone's calling was worked into the job so the individual might do more of what she loves and gets the chance to apply, stretch, and grow her inborn, beloved skill in new ways. One sales manager I met turned her deep passion for theater into a teaching class. She created role-playing classes for young sales reps, herself playing the role of five different types of retail buyers that they'd likely encounter on the job. She put great zeal into every performance to maximize the reality of the variety of scenarios and to maximize the quality of learning for her students. An energetic administrator I met fed her deeply held passion for event planning by volunteering to take the lead in handling the logistics of any and all pending big corporate events she came across. She enrolled her boss to actively look across the company for event-planning occasions, with an emphasis on new planning experiences that would allow her to learn more about the discipline of her calling, while still adding value to the company.

I personally have incorporated inspirational speaking into a variety of endeavors at my place of work in an attempt to bring maximum value to the workplace while simultaneously testing and stretching my motivational abilities and feeding my aspiration to inspire. The meaning created adds value *and* voracity of commitment to my place of work.

Why not encourage, mold, and reward all of this reimagining? Why not feed the need for learning and personal growth? Why not harness this desire to bring more value and to be more valued at work?

Doing so invites a higher level of performance, by definition.

It requires sitting down with employees and first setting ground rules and refreshing expectations for the core job. Then, the discussion can flow to (1) how best to mold and bend the edges of the job to incorporate more of what they love to do and (2) how to incorporate more interesting challenges in general that would enhance their skill set and the value they bring to the workplace. You can even help employees incorporate elements of their calling into their jobs to get the best of both worlds. The alternative, quitting the job to pursue the calling in its purest form, may be a path to meaningful bliss, but it also certainly poses its own set of risks and potential difficulties.

Consider the zookeeper, for example.

Two researchers, J. Stuart Bunderson of Washington University Olin Business School and Jeffrey Thompson of Brigham Young University, studied the double-edged nature of those who pursue their true calling. They posed the case of the zookeeper as an example of how doing what we feel we were meant to do can certainly have a downside. As a group, zookeepers are highly educated (82 percent have a college degree) but very poorly paid (average annual salary of $25,000 at the time of the study). Sixty-three percent rely on a second source of income. In fact, 56 percent volunteered for months or years to get into the profession. Furthermore, the field of zookeeping is not rich with advancement opportunities or status. The work can also be physically demanding, dangerous, and uncomfortable. Zookeepers are often on call, requiring a sacrifice of personal time. Yet the zookeepers in the study felt bound by a sense of duty, feeling they had no choice but to put up with the sacrifices and burdens to do what they felt they were meant to do.[19]

By no means am I suggesting that encouraging someone to pursue his calling head-on isn't an admirable or viable path toward enabling deeply relevant learning or achieving true meaning and fulfillment in one's work life. My point is that for many, perhaps most of us, this simply may not be a realistic option. An accountant who feels drawn to teaching may realistically not have the means to leave her accounting job, go back to school, and start over. Or she may not want to go all in because she still very much loves a lot of the elements of her current job.

We have the ability as meaning-making managers to help our employees avoid double-edged choices and instead creatively discover ways to build elements of a calling into their work lives. What's to prevent our accountant/teacher from holding classes during lunch hours for new hires on the most critical elements of accounting according to what firm X believes? What's to keep her boss from granting flextime and helping provide connections to small, local business owners she could consult and teach the basics of accounting to? One such manager/employee team I encountered did just that.

Now, I am certainly not implying that all callings ultimately have application to all work. The investment banker who loves teaching music may just have to derive meaning at work in other ways (ways I detail in this book). But the allure of one's calling is irrefutably powerful, so why not at least have the discussion with the employee and explore how to creatively incorporate one's confessed calling into the job?

You might be surprised at the possibilities for connectivity. The meaning-o-meter might actually break trying to measure the impact.

I hope you are getting the sense that job reimagining requires imagination. As a manager you unquestionably have the opportunity to instigate job reshaping for your employees, or alternatively you can embrace and harness the covert meaning-making activity that is already occurring.

However, what about for yourself?

Generally speaking, managers like you, with (by definition) at least some level of organizational power, must feel more at ease in reshaping their own jobs to maximize learning, growth, and fulfillment, right?

Not so much.

In fact, Jane Dutton's research shows just the opposite. Managers actually perceive many more issues in reimagining their jobs than lower-ranking employees. The responsibility for bottom-line results weighs heavy on the minds of management and creates a feeling that every single moment must be spent on delivering the results. There simply isn't time to do more of what you love at work in challenging new ways, or there is a feeling that because everyone is watching you can't send the wrong signal.[20] This sense of responsibility can shut down openness to incorporating enjoyable, stretching, productive activities that could actually further enhance the bottom-line results and set a great example for the troops.

In an interesting contrast, lower-ranking employees are much more comfortable altering their work environments and tasks and adjusting the expectations and nature of interactions with others. In general, because they have less autonomy and their jobs are more structured and defined, they can better discern when and how they can spend time on newly crafted work tasks that will supplement and enhance delivery of their core job requirements. Being a lower-level employee brings with it a greater sense of freedom as well, with fewer people watching you.[21]

There is something to be learned here for time-pressed and hyperaware managers. While the pressures of delivering results can be daunting, all-encompassing, and must always be job #1, smartly infusing a bit of the greater sense of freedom the lower-ranking employee feels can be powerful. "Demoting" yourself and rebalancing the total portfolio of work done is a method of promoting a greater sense of personal growth and meaning in the work itself and ensuring performance stays on an ever-upward trajectory.

Method 5: Promote Learning Exchanges

Learning organizations are in a continuous learning mode, constantly drawing insight from everything they do. They also draw from every member in the organization, encouraging participation in an energetic exchange of learning intended to amplify growth. When you establish such exchanges for your employees, you become a powerful contributor to the cause. To maximize effectiveness of learning exchanges, design them around these thoughtful experiences:

❑ *Learn from the past.* Learning exchanges are at their most powerful when designed to leverage institutional knowledge to avoid repeating mistakes and provide access to wisdom born from experience. The forum for so doing can take many forms, such as what I call "subsequent assessments," whereby a project or procedure is reviewed after execution or implementation in an effort to analyze and learn what worked/didn't work.

Learning from the past can also mean tapping into senior leaders and facilitating the sharing of their knowledge and wisdom. Getting senior leaders to share the little tips and tricks to success that their experience has taught them over the years can be incredibly valuable. Ever see someone with a little sign or Post-it note at their workspace with an inspiring nugget of wisdom written on it? Good chance it came from a senior leader's Top Ten List of keys to success or things learned on some leadership-related subject. One manager I interviewed orchestrated a series of connections with senior leaders, giving them the opportunity to share lessons learned from past experiences on a variety of topics. The manager then compiled the key nuggets into a menu of wisdom and disseminated it to his work group—instant insight to go.

Encouraging mentorship programs is another way to ensure that more experienced veterans get an outlet to share what they've learned from the past with a new generation of leaders.

Finally, flaunting failure is a great way to learn from the past and to ensure mistakes aren't repeated. Crafting situations where failures can be safely shared, without retribution, allows future learning to be gleaned from the past.

❏ *Escalate ideas.* Eve Mitleton-Kelly of the London School of Economics espouses the concept of co-evolution of ideas, the phenomenon that occurs during the learning process whereby individuals will influence each other and their ideas will co-evolve. The evolution happens as ideas adapt and change in the context of other ideas and exchange of knowledge, which, in turn, influences what happens next.[22] Creating learning exchanges to facilitate idea percolation can thus have a positive impact on the ultimate strength of the idea.

❏ *Develop an information-sharing habit.* One of the most basic but effective learning exchanges you can facilitate comes from the simple habit of sharing information with your organization and allowing for questions and dialogue in return. When information is shared on a regular basis across the organization, people's commitment to learning strengthens.[23] Share what you've personally learned or what the organization has learned and how it's being acted on. It can take the form of periodic town halls, staff meetings, or any number of mechanisms with two-way communication opportunities built in. The bottom line is that when your employees start from a base of being in the know, it spurs their desire to learn more and contribute more.

❏ *Share and reapply best practices.* Learning exchanges are also powerful when designed with the intent of sharing and reapplying best practices (or facilitating the rip-n-run, as one manager called it). Whether it's brown-bag lunch panels, shadowing, communal presentations, or any other tactic, sharing and reapplying means accelerating and elevating improved performance.

❏ *Provide the stimuli for discovery.* The element of discovery inherent in gaining new knowledge can make learning exchanges exciting. Discovery often requires new stimuli, something you can surely provide. Capability presentations from vendors, simulations, conferences, classroom training (with report-backs for broader audiences), and seminars are just some of the ways to help facilitate the exchange of interesting and relevant new learning.

Method 6: Make the Employee's Personal Learning a Priority

Roger Enrico, famed former CEO of Pepsi, a company with more than $30 billion in annual sales and 300,000 employees back in his day, spent more than 100 days a year conducting workshops for senior executives.[24]

You know where this is going.

If someone with the weight of a company on his mind can make that kind of investment in the learning and growth of his team, you can certainly take inspiration to declare your employees' personal learning a priority, at least at some level.

The first part is committing. Then, a learning plan can be created that congruently challenges the employee (thus triggering the second Marker of Meaning). Congruency comes into play when you maximize meaning for employees by introducing learning opportunities that align with what truly energizes them and maximizes the most highly relevant learning and growth. To unveil such learning opportunities, you and your employee can explore three questions, which are intended to serve as pillars on which to construct a thoughtful learning plan:

1. What do I need to learn to advance my career?

2. What do I want to learn that advances my cause?

3. What am I interested to learn to feed my curiosity?

Learning that adds to your employees' career progression efforts produces meaning by increasing their felt sense of competence and self-confidence, and by helping them to achieve a desired career objective—a source of meaning in and of itself. It also directly leads to peak performance. In fact, top performers are three times as likely as typical performers to plan their learning around where they want to go next in their career. Furthermore, top performers take approximately 40 percent more training hours than the employee average and are more likely than typical performers to do independent reading in their area of specialty.[25] So, when constructing a learning plan, start with a foundation that enables one's desired career advancement. Truly committing to this learning is directly linked to sustained elevated performance.

Learning that helps to feed one's purpose or desired legacy (the person's cause) is just as powerful. For example, if your stated purpose was to "unlock the potential of every person who works for you," then you should include in your learning plan some intentional effort to learn more about each employee in your shop. This personal knowledge could help you better tailor your approach and achieve your worthy goal. Learning that can help feed your purpose or desired legacy should be its own pillar in your learning plan.

Finally, feeding the desire to simply learn, to practice the art of life-long learning without reason other than obtaining new knowledge or skills, is worthy of its own pillar in the learning plan. Becoming a more knowledgeable version of ourselves is a tremendous source of meaning and fulfillment. And nurturing curiosity in your employees automatically increases their knowledge and experience base, contributing to the likelihood of elevated performance over time.

You're thinking that prioritizing all of this personal learning is great and all, but as managers, one of our primary responsibilities is to keep employees churning in a productive, efficient do-loop. It's good for the business—right?

Well, yes, to a certain extent.

However, at some point, to inject more meaning into a workplace and orchestrate higher-performance levels, we have to help others get out of the do-loop and into a learning-loop.

Prioritizing personal learning can be difficult to do—full stop. We've all walked a mile here. It's so easy to get caught up in the daily responsibilities of our jobs that learning opportunities are often the first thing to go. Figure 5-1 is a visual reminder of the importance of breaking out of the cycle of day-to-day doing to evolve into a cycle of commitment to learning. It forces us to be cognizant of when we are trapped in a cycle of merely doing and to then intentionally move to a more productive cycle of both doing and learning.

Figure 5-1. The do-loop versus the learning loop.

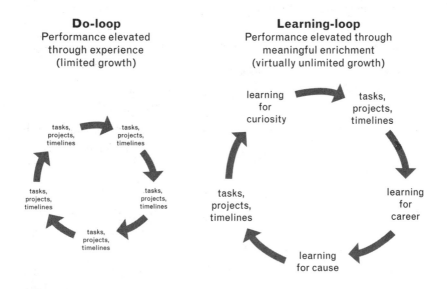

The do-loop (see Figure 5-1) illustrates the vicious cycle of getting caught in a never-ending flow of tasks, projects, and timelines. The circular shape itself represents our learning and growth at work. The size of the circle equates to the amount of learning and growth we can expect in such an environment—relatively stunted in this case, as evidenced by the small size of the circle. In contrast, the learning-loop shows the virtuous cycle of starting with one's core job (tasks, projects, and timelines), but intentionally interspersing the sources of congruent learning and growth in between the pure focus on the daily duties. The size of the circle is proportionally much larger, indicating the virtually unlimited amount of learning and growth at our disposal when we get into a highly relevant and energizing learning-loop. The difference in the size of the two circles in Figure 5-1 also depicts the difference in the depth of meaning and fulfillment and height of performance between the two scenarios. The learning-loop is drawn to scale, so you should be drawn to scale up your efforts to create such a loop.

Method 7: Lean Forward to Learn

Diane Dietz, chief marketing officer of grocery giant Safeway and Whirlpool board member, encourages you to get off your recliner. Dietz explains:

> When people are really comfortable, they are in their home zone—sitting in their La-Z-Boy. They might be comfortable, but the truth is there's very little learning taking place. When people step too far out of their comfort zone, they step into their panic zone. Little learning takes place here because instincts kick in, people panic, and they just want to go home. The key is to land right of center, just on the edge of your panic zone. It's a little scary, but this is where truly meaningful, motivating learning lives.

You can show your employees the way. Seek out a new learning experience for yourself that stretches you and make a point of sharing your experience with your employees. Encourage them to get out of their own comfort zone and lean into something new and even daunting (but short of their panic zone, of course). Applying the techniques you've learned in this chapter will help employees feel safe in so doing.

The effort is worth it because when we lean forward to learn, there's no holding back our potential or potential fulfillment.

* * *

The development of an effective learning and growth environment does not have to be a complex undertaking, but it does require a structured and intentional approach. And much of the required structure and intentionality comes down to your desire to elevate learning and growth on your personal agenda, and on your performance agenda.

CHAPTER 6

Meaningful Decision Making and Influence

A GOOD DECISION-MAKING PROCESS IS AS MUCH ABOUT THE PRO-
cess as the decision because it is a way to enable people to contribute
directly to and feel integral to an operation. Research consistently
shows that work comes to be meaningful when individuals see themselves as capable of substantively influencing outcomes. It's meaningful because it tells them they are not powerless and that they have the
ability to make a real difference.[1]

Unfortunately, the desire for a sense of contribution all too often
goes unmet in today's workplace. A global workforce study by Towers
Watson showed that, overall, only 39 percent of respondents agreed
their organization's management effectively involved employees in
decisions that affected them. And about the same low percentage
agreed their organization solicited and acted on employees' suggestions and input. In stark contrast, among those identified as "highly
engaged," more than 66 percent agreed their organization solicited and
acted on employees' input and suggestions.[2]

Research also shows that allowing employees to participate in managerial decisions also positively impacts job satisfaction, organizational
commitment, labor-management relations, job performance and organizational performance, employee absenteeism, and profits.[3]

As managers in control of how decisions get made, we can directly enable the fourth Marker of Meaning and grant others the feeling of being in control and able to influence decisions/outcomes as well as give them a sense of autonomy—all of which contributes to meaning-making and a sense of self-discovery. Decision making is not just a process for making the call and getting employees focused on what matters; it is a *philosophy* for helping employees matter more.

EMPLOYEE-CENTERED DECISION MAKING

I know what you might be thinking.

Involving employees in the decision-making process is great and all, but we have a business to run. Sometimes you've just got to make the call. It's efficient. It's quick. And shouldn't the more experienced point of view drive the decision?

All true.

There are plenty of instances where directive leadership and decision making is required. For example, Dr. Keith Hmieleski from Texas Christian University found that overly involving employees in decision making in an environment of particularly fast-paced change can lead to organizational chaos. "Fast-moving environments demand fast decisions," says Hmieleski.[4]

As managers we should be able to intuitively sense when we are operating in the kind of environment where the call just has to be made, or where involving employees is just not practical or appropriate. However, we are talking here about everyday decision making, and a powerful philosophy that can be converted into a practice of substantive meaning for employees.

The method of centering decision-making processes on employees allows those employees to contribute their best, grow the most, and feel worthwhile and worthy. And it's a practice that means these employees will better commit to the decision and own the problems born from the decision, as well as be driven to prove the decision correct. It also means the involved employees will learn how to more effectively make their own decisions when called upon, and be better able to focus without the distraction of distrust that comes with being handed decisions.

The construction of a decision-making process, then, should have as its foundation well-thought-through mechanisms for putting the employees firmly into the mix.

Lehigh Valley Health Network in Pennsylvania subscribes to this philosophy and exercises employee-involved decision making accordingly, taking it all the way to flowing substantial freedom of choice to the front lines—nurses. Nurses are given a strong voice in determining nursing routines, standards, and quality of care and are given a lot of leeway to make bedside decisions. The intense satisfaction this generates among the staff landed it on the Fortune 100 Best Places to Work list three consecutive years. In fact, *Fortune* noted the robust culture of involving staff in decision making as a prime reason for the hospital making the list.[5]

So the question becomes how to convert a potent, employee-centric philosophy into great practice. To do so, let's start with an important insight.

Decision-making processes can unchain instead of drain energy if built from the point of view of those most affected by the decision (versus being built solely from the point of view of the decider). Employee-centered decision making flips the standard process on its head by viewing things first through the lens of the frontline employees that are most often affected by the decision.

A METHOD FOR EMPLOYEE-CENTERED DECISION MAKING

I've developed a step-by-step method for how to continually and thoughtfully place employees at the center of decision making to maximize the meaning and fulfillment they derive from the process (and to still arrive at effective decisions, of course). Follow these seven steps:

Step 1: Fulfill the Foundational Requirements

When we seek to move the locus of control to one that's shared with employees, there are some basic requirements that we first have to ensure are met. John Jacob Gardiner, professor of leadership at Seattle University, indicates that the top-two characteristics necessary for a genuine process of shared governance are a climate of trust and a commitment to information sharing (disclosing data necessary for quality decision making).[6]

Trust comes from the investment you've made in your employees, and sharing information is a habit you simply must develop, as Chapter 5 points out. Another foundational requirement is the establishment of decision criteria based on clear objectives and a keen understanding of each person's role in the decision-making process. Clarifying each person's role in decision making can be as simple as specifically identifying who owns the process of facilitating the decision, being clear on who actually gets to make the decision, who gets to give input, and who has to go execute the decision. Being clear on roles can help eliminate the all-too-common chaos that can occur when people think they have authority to decide or veto, but they really don't.

Step 2: Hold a Decision Stakeholders Meeting

Get together with everyone involved in a decision. Confirm the decision criteria, objectives, roles, and responsibilities established as part of the foundational requirements. Identify resources to support the decision-making team and set milestones as well.

Employees want an efficient and organized method for bringing their ideas, input, and analysis to influence decisions. And they want clarity on what's required to make a decision. The best way to honor their time and commitment is to provide this clarity and streamline the process as much as possible at the initial stage. You'll avoid random, unnecessary, or repetitive requests for supporting data or analysis later, all of which can bring about frustration instead of the fulfillment that a thoughtful decision-making process can bring.

Step 3: Ask for a Recommendation

One of the best ways to involve employees in decision making in an enriching fashion is to give them time and space to think options through, cast their own critical eye on those options, form their own recommendations about those options, and then share those options with a decision-making body.

It's amazing how often managers bypass this opportunity.

If a team is involved in the options analysis, it's not as important that the team members come in with an aligned recommendation as it is that they've clearly thought through pros and cons, and that each individual has had a chance to fully develop and share his thinking in an effort to influence. So while people need to weigh in before they can buy in, they also want a chance to think through, then sell through.

Kip Olmstead, onetime chief marketing officer at Crayola, is a staunch believer in making sure everyone with the wherewithal to influence a decision gets heard and is comfortable sharing thoughts and recommendations in the process. Olmstead described for me his belief as such:

> I actively seek out the lone wolfs that might be timid or nervous to share their point of view. They are often worried how they will be seen. I try to put them at ease. I ensure them that even in cases where they are not actually empowered to make the decision itself, or in cases where they may not feel empowered for whatever reason—especially younger folks—they are absolutely empowered to share their opinion and recommendation. I openly want different opinions. As Patton said: "If everyone is thinking the same way, then no one is thinking." Then I try to role-model really listening. I often ask, if you were the CEO of this decision, what would you do?

Ryan McLean, general manager/VP at Bissell (a major cleaning products company), told me:

> The single biggest thing we do here to involve employees in the decision and create empowerment is push the recommendation as far down the organization as possible. The person absolutely closest to the action writes the recommendation, presenting options and pros and cons along with it. The management team really focuses and listens intently to that recommendation. We hear back consistently from the presenters what a meaningful, fulfilling experience it is for them. They tell us they felt like they were part of the decision-making process in a truly meaningful fashion, not as an afterthought.

Olmstead and McLean clearly place a premium on encouraging employees to formulate and share their thoughts and recommendations, and on visibly listening to and acting on those recommendations as appropriate.

You can do the same.

And when you do, you give your employees a chance to learn and grow by developing their thinking and communication, you show them they are valued and valuable, and you forge stronger relationships with them—all meaningful outcomes.

By the way, my experience tells me that you will also arrive at a better decision 99 times out of 100.

Step 4: Conduct Inquiries, Not Inquisitions

Meaning and fulfillment derived from involvement in decision making quickly evaporates when a decision-making body turns an opportunity for thoughtful inquiries into an inquisition. This happens when decision makers present questions to an informing body with an off-putting accusatory or condescending tone that comes across as seeking to undermine versus seeking to understand (it's the "you have to get past us" mentality). To avoid an atmosphere of inquisition, managers on the receiving end of options and recommendations can ask good questions and listen well with an obvious intent of understanding, while being certain to show appreciation for the thinking behind the points of view being presented.

The idea here is to let respect, intellectual honesty, curiosity, and a desire to comprehend drive the line of questioning versus trying to catch someone in the wrong. And again, limiting the requests for incremental data and analysis to the most important few at this stage, and explaining why these requests are warranted, can also help this interactive step feel like thoughtful inquiry instead of an inquisition.

Step 5: Debate. Decide. Commit.

Employees deserve a chance to be at the center of healthy debate in a healthy environment. Seattle University's Gardiner points out that employees involved in a decision have to feel protected when bringing any divergent points of view forward.[7] Otherwise it's destroying the meaning derived from being involved in the decision-making process to begin with. So varying viewpoints should be protected and respected and input carefully and visibly considered. This will further energize the employee's desire to inform and influence decisions.

Then when it's time to decide, it's time to decide—period. In fact, one of the quickest ways a manager can drain meaning for those involved in a decision-making process is to *not* make the call and dither over various options. It's one of the most thoughtful things you can do as a manager; employees just want the decision made after they've shared their point of view. Even those who might not agree with the call will derive satisfaction from the focus that comes from a decision simply being made.

Not to be forgotten, the decisions themselves should be weighed and made transparently without hidden agendas (which rarely remain hidden, in truth). It is extremely unfulfilling to present your case only to have facts and arguments glossed over and preexisting motivations clearly driving the decision. Decision makers should spell out why they are deciding what they are while recognizing differing points of view in the process so that everyone knows they were heard.

Finally, the decision maker should ask for commitment to the decision, pointing out the opportunity for a further sense of esprit de corps behind a united front of support, and stressing that the mission won't succeed without total commitment, from everyone—especially given the barriers that will certainly arise in an increasingly competitive business world.

The U.S. Army Ranger School teaches the lesson of commitment in a resounding fashion. Rangers are expected to accomplish their mission despite all obstacles, and given the relatively small size of a Ranger unit, everyone must be fully committed to the mission and execute with excellence to achieve their goal. One Ranger I interviewed told me of getting ambushed and "killed" as the platoon leader of his unit during a simulated raid in the harrowing two-month trial, so he was thus unable to participate in a critical raid behind enemy lines in the later stages of the course.

Expecting the Ranger instructor to tell him he had failed the course, he instead was told he passed with flying colors. He was reminded that he was the platoon leader responsible for ensuring the *platoon* successfully accomplished the mission, which they were able to do despite his untimely death. Why? Because he had fully enrolled everyone in his unit to the mission and specific plan, and then inspired fierce commitment to both. That commitment held the unit together and kept them on task all the way through to successful completion of the mission, through the most extreme, trying conditions imaginable, and even without their leader in tow.[8]

As you lead your own platoon on the front lines of business, instilling fierce commitment can help overcome any obstacle, leading to enriching success.

Step 6: Ensure Energy-Yielding Outcomes

After all the effort and energy that goes into making a high-quality, employee-centered decision, the outcomes should return the energy back into the system. This energy can take the form of an organization visibly acting on decisions and sticking to them over the long haul and seeing decisions communicated quickly and broadly to all those affected (while providing a chance for clarifying questions to be asked). Focus and even a sense of pride from a good, fair decision are other positive outcomes. Positive energy and gratification can also take the form of feedback from the decider on how the involved employees specifically contributed to the shaping of a solid, well-informed decision.

Step 7: Conduct a Decision Quality Check

A postmortem on a sample of decisions made can bring enrichment through retrospection. Was the right decision made? (Who was right or wrong doesn't matter, by the way.) Did people stick to the decision? What could/should have been known to make a better decision? Relishing a decision well made and looking to learn from decisions made and the process undertaken to get to those decisions can contribute to a felt sense of competence and confidence in decision making, which in turn encourages continued commitment to a fulfilling employee-centered approach.

* * *

The method I've laid out can thoughtfully and effectively enable employees to take part in influencing and making decisions—such that it's a fulfilling experience along the way.

So, what about when the employee isn't just a participant in a decision, but is the proprietor of the decision? Let's take a look now at how to maximize meaning by delegating the decision making from management down to the employees.

INTELLIGENT AUTONOMY

What do President Obama and heavy metal guitarist Yngwie Malm-steen have in common?

They both wear essentially the same thing every day so that they can save their brainpower for bigger, more important decisions.

Constantly making decisions can strain a decision maker—so the opportunity to share the decision-making space can be quite appealing. And if involving employees in decision making is meaningful to them, then enabling them to actually make the decision will be exponentially more important. The key is to create "intelligent autonomy" that gives employees the independence and influence they crave, but does so in a manner that thoughtfully avoids the contradictions and pitfalls of a poorly executed delegation of power.

And there are plenty of such pitfalls to avoid, which we'll get to in a bit.

First, let's gain an appreciation for the astounding power of auton-omy done right. According to a report by the *Journal of Personality and Social Psychology*, the number-one contributor to happiness in life is not money, popularity, good looks, or even a good sex life. It's auton-omy: "the feeling that your life—its activities and habits—are self-chosen and self-endorsed."[9]

Research clearly shows that jobs allowing for higher levels of auton-omy have been shown to generate more meaning at work.[10]

University of Michigan professor Gretchen Spreitzer conducted a study of twenty years of research on empowerment at work and found that empowered employees report a high level of job satisfaction and organizational commitment, lower turnover, increased performance effectiveness, and increased motivation. Relatedly, supervisors who reported higher levels of empowerment were seen by their subordi-nates as more innovative, upward influencing, and inspirational.[11] Empowerment executed effectively also engenders meaningful out-comes like increased trust and bonding between the giver and receiver, and an elevated sense of ownership, control, self-esteem, and accom-plishment for those empowered.

Position power gives way to personal power with autonomy.

Research indicates that when employees have greater levels of autonomy, they are better able to use their personal attributes to contribute to job performance—a deeply satisfying and rewarding experience.[12] For example, I've witnessed an empowered manager drive a critical but controversial project to an effective conclusion by using her unique talents of skilled listening and empathy to persuade misaligned key stakeholders. Her manager would have achieved the same outcome, but undoubtedly would have left a trail of bodies in his wake. The empowered was able to succeed by doing it "her way" and got a chance to exercise traits that are core to her value system—a meaningful experience through and through.

So given all this goodness, how can you craft intelligent autonomy, or empowerment done right?

It starts with a simple but important insight: It takes work to give away work.

This is particularly true if you want to avoid the surprising dark side of empowerment. Here are eight ways to grant autonomy in an intelligent fashion—each method overcomes a specific pitfall, which is also described.

1. *Fulfill the foundational requirements.* Similar to the employee-centered decision-making method, intelligent autonomy requires a baseline of trust and a practice of information sharing. An additional foundational requirement for successfully implementing autonomy rests on the manager's willingness to delegate growth work, not just grunt work. Employees have to feel themselves stretching and feel the influence they have to truly feel empowered. If you allow for substantive, not inconsequential decisions to be made by the empowered, and overcome any fear you might have of delegating some big decisions as well, you are on the way to smartly implementing autonomy and avoiding some of the most basic pitfalls en route.

So what is the right balance? What is the right amount of decision-making power and autonomy to transfer to the employee(s)? Empowerment expert Mac McIntire uses an analogy that's brilliant (literally) to provide helpful perspective for the manager who wants to get it right:

Empowering employees is analogous to the process of sending power through a light bulb. If 100 watts of power is sent through a 10-watt bulb, the bulb will blow up. If 10 watts of power is sent through a 100-watt bulb, the bulb will glow dimly and not achieve its full capacity. Likewise, if 100 watts of empowerment is sent through a 10-watt employee, the manager may fry the brain of the employee. Some employees cannot handle more than a few watts of responsibility and authority. Empowering these employees with a surge of new responsibilities may cause sudden spasms of anxiety and rapid burnout. On the other hand, if a manager sends 10 watts of empowerment through a 100-watt employee (one who is fully capable and willing to do more), the employee will never achieve his or her full potential. Highly capable employees who are underutilized become de-energized when their talents and abilities are not used fully. Eventually, 100-watt employees who are only given 10 watts of power either become 10-watt employees or they leave the company and go somewhere where they can reach their full potential.[13]

So size up the amount of power transference the employee can handle and let the empowerment wattage flow. Don't underestimate the wattage of each employee (there are very few 10-watt-bulb employees in reality), and take pride in the number of 100-watt employees shining to their fullest potential in your shop.

2. *Have an agreement for autonomy in place.* Has a manager ever told you that he's empowering you with something, and you catch yourself thinking, "Yeah, right"?[14] This happens when the manager's agreement to empower is continually violated by his actions.

Peter Mills of the University of Oregon and Gerardo Ungson of San Francisco State have discovered that managers often struggle with the empowerment of subordinates, seeing it only as a loss of their own power. Their compensating behaviors in the wake of this realization leave the empowered actually feeling more scrutiny, which results in the complete opposite effect of what was intended—the loss of a sense of competence, confidence, and thus meaning.[15]

Or perhaps the manager dives right in at the first sign of trouble and takes over, or he empowers without giving any direction, expectations, guidance, or operating parameters—which makes you feel like he's dumping, not delegating. As Oxford professor, director of research, and empowerment expert Conrad Lashley told me, "Empowerment or participative management is not universally accepted and will fail if employees are ill prepared and the process of participation is arbitrary and poorly managed."[16]

To avoid frustrating employees with false autonomy, develop an Agreement for Autonomy. Whether a document or a discussion, it will formalize the rules of engagement and operation in the handover of power. Such an agreement can be broken out into three parts: construction, consideration, and consultation.

Construction involves building a basic set of expectations for the work associated with the empowered task(s). It is here that you agree on the specific objective and desired goals behind the delegated work, as well as reach an understanding of the specific work that needs to be done, decisions that need to be made, and the success measures that will determine if the transferred power was wielded effectively to achieve the desired end-goal. You also establish clear parameters around the scope of the autonomy given. Parameters greatly reduce the likelihood of you worrying about the empowered going too far and overstepping their decision-making authority. A fair enough concern on your behalf, by the way, because the fact is that when autonomy is implemented well, the empowered have the authority to do their jobs—not yours.[17] When clear boundaries are set, it is time to forge connections between you and the empowered through consideration and consultation.

Consideration means that employees who are fully empowered to make certain decisions must also show some specific consideration toward the delegator (you), such as keeping you informed. You will then be able to back up your employees' decisions if necessary, and you can better answer inquiries from your own chain of command. Informed managers are also less nervous managers. You'll be less tempted to intercede when you have information to keep you in check.

Consultation spells out the decisions that will require your specific consultation. You need to be brave in pushing the authority to make decisions down into the organization while still having a mechanism for giving your input if it's truly necessary. Consultation allows your employees a chance to own some particularly tricky or vital decisions they may not otherwise have been able to make (again, as long as you hold to letting them make the call and are fully supportive afterward). The opportunity to consult with you, when warranted, can also increase the odds that the empowered will make wise decisions, which can further boost their self-confidence in decision making farther down the line. Finally, having an expectation for consultation in certain instances can also serve as a lifeline to overcome one of the most damaging reasons that we might be reluctant to hand over power—when we feel threatened and fear we will wind up becoming irrelevant. If an opportunity to consult can ease this fear and avoid the corresponding contradictory behavior, all the better. Just start from a place of being brave and being very selective in assessing which situations truly necessitate a consult.

3. *Facilitate recipient readiness.* Just because employees are empowered doesn't mean they are set up to succeed. They may have difficulty accepting the new responsibilities for fear they will be overmatched or because they view the new responsibilities as an added burden to a job that already has enough pressures. As a countermeasure to this unhealthy set of attitudes, you must ensure that your employees are ready to accept the responsibility. Provide training and resources; have a discussion with them about the benefits of the newfound autonomy. You should work to ease the fears of accountability that can come with empowerment, ensuring that people are set up to win and confident that they will. The employees themselves have to demonstrate that they are ready, willing, and able as well.

4. *Provide intrinsic and extrinsic reward.* More work without more reward is rarely welcome. And even if the work must be done, the motivation might not exist to do it. That is why it is so vital to ensure that there are intrinsic and extrinsic rewards baked into the new work. You can make the work intrinsically motivating by building in flexibility to allow employees to define what they want to get out of the new autonomy granted. Let employees choose their own goals to go with the agreed-on objectives, or even help them brainstorm what's in it for them that could be very personally rewarding. Perhaps they want to use the newly transferred power to develop their leadership skills and decision-making capabilities. They may be interested in growing their ability to develop other people, increasing the rapport with their cross-functional partners, or just learning something new for the pleasure of learning.

Studies consistently show that goals we choose for ourselves are the most powerful at driving motivation, satisfaction, creativity, resilience, and performance.[18] You can also make work intrinsically motivating by building in choice. When autonomy is granted, freedom of choice should be automatically included, on as many vectors as possible.

The video game industry could teach us something here. Premieres of mega-selling video games are now bigger than the biggest movie premieres, and the industry shows no signs of slowing down. In 2013, *Grand Theft Auto V*, the fifth installment in a wildly popular gaming franchise, reached $1 billion in sales in just three days, making it the biggest entertainment launch in history, by a long shot. (It took nineteen days for the movie *The Avengers* to reach the $1 billion mark.) The game is known for the expansive number of choices it offers the gamer and for the variety of ways gamers can achieve their goal and have fun.[19] In fact, you don't even have to play the game's plot to have fun. You can spend hours just randomly exploring, marauding, and doing stunts.

The correlation between choice and the astonishing sales of the game are hardly a coincidence. In fact, video game designers have long been studying the psychology of choice and its role in maintaining engagement. The thrill of exercising autonomous decision making helps to explain the explosion of this incredibly absorbing hobby and industry.[20]

Intrinsic reward is also fueled by encouraging employees to pursue ideas they are passionate about. Supporting passion-fueled ideas that autonomous workers develop is like energy feeding energy. The risk of the employee being wrong or not having the best possible idea is often outweighed by the excellence in execution, the infectious attitude experienced along the way, and the self-esteem points the employee will accumulate pursuing an idea with passion and vigor.

Of course, let us not forget the good old-fashioned *extrinsic* reward and recognition that should accompany the added responsibility and accountability sought from the employee. Proper recognition for expanded responsibility that is well handled is a must, as are meaningful rewards (covered in Chapter 7).

5. *Facilitate by assisting success versus avoiding failure.* Mistakes will be made when employees are given autonomy. Part of the reason employees need to be empowered in the first place is to learn from the experience of their mistakes. The mistake you have to avoid as a manager is reacting poorly to their mistakes. It's important that you let the cycle of empowerment work itself out where the employee learns from both successes and failures. You have to act as a facilitator, not a fixer, and allow delegated decisions to stick (and even help them to stick with higher authorities and broader-reaching groups). It's equally important that you wholeheartedly demonstrate the belief that the empowered can handle the added responsibilities without incessant oversight. The minute you start acting like you want people to avoid any miscues, the empowerment itself has failed.

Instead, shift to a mindset of assisting success. Help your empowered employees move quickly past mistakes as needed, and then turn your energy back to finding ways to help them succeed.

6. *Construct communication loops.* Breakdowns in communication can mean a breakdown in trust between you and the employee you've delegated decision-making authority to. Autonomous employees shouldn't go off the grid, but instead should find ways to report back regularly on progress. Checkpoints should be established (as part of the *consideration* portion of the agreement for autonomy) to provide updates, encouragement, help, training in teachable moments, and to avoid operational drift whereby work migrates away from previously aligned objectives and parameters. For example, I once witnessed an empowered but disconnected group of engineers slowly "lose the plot" and begin to chase an exciting objective, but one materially different from the original. Enormous amounts of time, money, and effort were wasted when they finally checked back in with the delegator only to discover they had entirely overdesigned the wrong mousetrap.

And while those working autonomously can't forget to check in, you can't just delegate and check out, either. Communication needs to be a two-way street. It can put your mind at ease as well as help the confidence of the autonomously operating individuals as they feel better connected.

7. *Covet communication loops.* A study by Kurt Dirks of the Olin Business School at Washington University revealed that high levels of psychological ownership resulting from autonomy can cause resistance to change and low levels of cooperation (a "stay out of my sandbox" mentality).[21] For example, an empowered team of researchers may be operating effectively but in turn develop such a strong identity that they bristle at a simple requested change in research protocol or, worse, may come to view all inquiries from their chain of command as mere interferences. Not a healthy viewpoint from anyone's perspective.

To preempt this phenomenon, communicate with your empowered employees so that they actually come to *covet* the communication loops in place over time, viewing them as helpful and rewarding. When you begin to sense that the fierce sense of independence developed is beginning to backfire, it's time to revisit how the communication loops are being used. Focusing those communication touch points on open, honest, helpful, and rewarding exchanges can leave the empowered feeling that it is productive and powerful to continue inviting management in along the way as appropriate.

8. *Tie a measurement tether.* Establishing success criteria and measures in the agreement for autonomy and reviewing progress against those measures periodically (as part of the communication loop) will help ensure work stays on course. It also helps keep the empowered motivated along the way as they have tangible evidence they are on track to hitting their goal. As important, keeping the measures front and center reinforces what success looks like; otherwise it can easily fall prey to a variety of interpretations.

For example, research conducted at a large organization sought to confirm the relationship between employee health and work performance. You'd expect the relationship to be obvious: Poor health would correlate with poor performance. But surprisingly, the research showed that across all gradients of reported health (and there were definite known health issues at this company), self-assessed performance remained high. Follow-up on the study indicated the source of contradiction—all the employees in the study regarded themselves as high-performing because they were "doing what they were told." Compliance was viewed as success, a sentiment not shared by management.[22]

Having agreed-on measurements in place and keeping them at the forefront ensures everyone defines success the same way and helps ensure that the ultimate output of the autonomy can be celebrated by all—which is meaningful in its own right.

*　*　*

You can't sustain intelligent autonomy on autopilot, but the effort invested will automatically bring a return in engagement, performance, and fulfillment.

Likewise, you can help employees matter more by engaging them in decision making, which brings more meaning.

And deciding to help employees matter more should be one of the easiest decisions you'll ever make.

part four

DEVOTION

CHAPTER 7

Cultures of Consequence

THERE IS A COMMON MISCONCEPTION THAT A COMPANY'S CUL-
ture is something to address once the fundamentals of performance are
sound. The truth is, as work culture researcher Douglas Stewart found,
if you want to change the performance of an organization, start with its
cultural norms. Norms, attitudes, and beliefs that the workers adopt
reflect directly on the organization's performance. For example, an
organization where people say, "Around here, you've got to watch your
back and don't make waves" produces very different results than one
where you hear people say, "Around here, everyone really cares about
each other and the quantity and quality of work we output together."[1]
Accordingly, establishing a cultural norm that connects employees to
one another and inspires a drive for greater achievement must be
viewed as a fundamental for long-term, sustained success.

Harvard Professors John Kotter and James Heskett proved the
impact an organization's culture can have on performance in a study
that analyzed 200 companies over an eleven-year period—the most
comprehensive and decisive such study ever conducted. They found
that companies that put energy into creating a performance-enhancing
culture drove revenue 765 percent higher versus just one percent higher
over the same period for companies without such a focus.[2]

So the key is to invest in a winning, performance-enhancing culture—but not just any kind will do.

For example, cultures that promote innovation, risk taking, and creativity certainly drive performance, as do cultures of accountability. All are great approaches.

The distinction to be made here, though, is whether the tenets of a culture drive performance in a way that *profits everyone*—the company and all its constituents. Does the culture propel performance in a way that maximizes daily meaning derived and fulfillment experienced for each of its members? Cultures that are rich in meaning manifestation generate feelings of significance, genuineness, belonging, and expanding personal potential—they are cultures of consequence. This approach *sustains* elevated performance over time.

How a company changes its culture also matters. Cultural change isn't as easy as flipping a switch, but leaders, nonetheless, often think they can simply dictate culture. They soon learn they cannot, but not before giving cultural change a bad reputation. Leaders absolutely can and should put the right practices in place and set an example, but the organization itself must be driven to change something like culture. This motivation comes when people can *feel* meaning being introduced into the workplace. They can see the benefits and understand intrinsically why adopting a culture of consequence is so right once they begin to experience it. The combination of both a role-modeling leader and a willing organization leads to cultural change.

So what does a meaning-rich, performance-driving culture of consequence actually look like? Dig into and study any Great Workplaces list and you'll uncover the three elements that the most meaning-rich cultures have in common: caring, authenticity, and teamwork.

A workplace's culture firmly shapes the way employees show up every day and can boost or drain the baseline energy level. Cultures built on caring, authenticity, and teamwork go one better and serve as a wellspring of meaning and fulfillment that employees draw from every day. This type of culture, in turn, further enhances sustained performance as deeply committed and interconnected employees are highly motivated to perform individually and as a group. It sets norms of behavior that produces results.

Building such a culture directly triggers the fifth Marker of Meaning—the desire to work in a compassionate, genuine, team-oriented environment where people feel appreciated, able to bring their whole true selves to work, and where the sense of harmony and belongingness with coworkers, leaders, and the company is palpable.

Let's take a closer look at each element.

CARING

Three of the Nehemiah Manufacturing Company's employees are beaming. They are talking about their experience at the company. Shawn Spradley says he wants to retire from Nehemiah. Clifton Misbetl passionately states he has loved his first seven months on the job—using the word *loved* five times. Michael Taylor says he loves coming to work every single day—and he especially likes seeing his friends at work. The intensity of conviction with which they speak of their company isn't the only thing unusual at work here.

When Clifton started his first day, he entered Nehemiah's door from the streets—homeless. Shawn Spradley landed a job at Nehemiah after a very long search that was inhibited by his drug-related felonious past. Michael Taylor got a job at Nehemiah after being kicked out of several temp jobs once his background check and troubled past came up.

This consumer packaged goods company (and provider of contract manufacturing services for a variety of brands) is no ordinary company. Its mission is very different, rooted in a startling philosophy. As CEO Dan Meyer puts it:

> We are about building brands, creating jobs, and changing lives.
> We believe the company exists to serve the people, not the other
> way around. It's about love, hope, and caring for the community.
> Everyone wants to feel loved and be a part of something bigger.
> Love, teamwork, and being part of a family—we really believe

that. We're trying to rebuild a little piece of the community one
piece at a time.

Nehemiah is a company fundamentally rooted in caring. It hires
previously overlooked employees with troubled pasts in an effort to
give them a second chance and is continually blown away by how these
supposedly at-risk employees turn out to be amazing contributors.
That doesn't happen without help, of course: Nehemiah provides the
environment for these second-chance employees to thrive, rooted in
the deepest levels of caring. "

Dan Meyer is out on the floor every day, twice a day, just checking
in to see how we are doing. He makes you feel welcome. He knows all of
our stories. I first met Dan out on the assembly line and I had no idea
who he was. I couldn't believe it when I found out later he was the CEO,"
said Taylor.

Fellow assembly-line worker Angela McDonald added, "This is a
family here—a true family. It's amazing what they are willing to do for
us. And they listen to your ideas, no matter who you are. They care
enough to really listen."

Showing up as really caring is part of Nehemiah's DNA. As Meyer
says, "It's not about what you say. I can tell everyone all day how much
I care. It's about what you do."

And Nehemiah does a lot to show how much it cares, despite
being only a modestly profitable startup so far. The company provides
clothes for those who don't have any as they enter the workforce
(some for the first time in quite a while). It provides free summer Fri-
day barbeques and monthly winter luncheons, interest-free loans for
those in need, Christmas bonuses and hams and turkeys at Thanks-
giving, Target gift cards on occasion, and even profit sharing when the
company overships production quotas. The generous and caring spirit
inspires the workers. Meyer confirms the intent: "Every person has
greatness inside," he says. "I try to bring it out—it's about caring
enough to really connect."

Meyer's very personal actions speak volumes as well. He has sometimes given employees rides to work. He intervened on behalf of a

worker and his drug use while ensuring the worker that he still had a job. He has had teary-eyed heart-to-hearts with employees in the parking lot. He discovered the ripple effect of extending a helping hand when Spradley's entire family thanked him at a church outing for "saving Shawn." This is the impact of a company whose very existence is based on the idea of caring.

Imagine if every company, every manager, operated as if it existed for the same sole reason.

What if we viewed the company as an entity intended simply for the betterment and enrichment of the human race, rather than the other way around?

Unfortunately, most of us aren't blessed with the chance to work in a startup that makes profits for the sole purpose of giving them back to the much-in-need employees.

However, that doesn't mean aspiring architects can't let the story of Nehemiah Manufacturing inspire them to build a core of caring into their meaning-rich culture. Doing so will most certainly unlock newfound levels of inner-connectedness among employees, who will feel as if they are part of something special. It will generate a deep sense of belongingness, which feeds a fundamental source of meaning for human beings. Building a core of caring into a culture will also elevate morale, as well as deliver returns for the company. Jim Goodnight, CEO of SAS, a business analytics firm that for two years in a row was recognized as *Fortune* magazine's number-one company to work for in America, says, "Treat employees as if they make a difference, and they will."[3]

Furthermore, organizational behavior and theory professors Tom Lawrence and Sally Maitlis say that the practice of nurturing a caring culture and caring relationships will also boost the workforce's resilience, helping employees to overcome adversity without being paralyzed or distracted.[4] Such resilience is critical to sustaining elevated performance over time.

The creation of a caring culture requires designing for and delivering on the five Components of Caring.

Family Unit—Not Military Unit

We return to the Army again as a source of insight, but view it from a different lens this time. In an Army unit, the "brass" socially distance themselves from the troops so they don't get unduly influenced when it comes time to make tough choices and/or send the troops into harm's way. Likewise, there is a respect for distance from authority put in place by the foot soldiers. As the soldiers say, "You can't mix the Os and Es" (officers and enlisted).

Preventing fraternization makes sense—for the military.

This arm's-length approach doesn't really work in the business world if you want to create meaning-filled connections and maximize elevated performance over the long haul. Thinking and acting like a family unit, where relationships and connections are a priority, is a better way. If you stop and think about the attributes of a happy family, you'll soon realize the number of traits that would be applicable for creation of a close-knit group in the workplace. And while each unhappy corporate family is unhappy in its own way, happy corporate families are all very similar. They and their employees:

* Make heartfelt connections with one another, showing warmth and an interest to connect.

* Openly and honestly communicate (even overcommunicate) with one another.

* Believe that "we're all in this together" and watch one another's back .

* Are fiercely committed to each other and put each other first.

* Share goals and values, and uphold family codes.

* Enjoy each other.

* Have compassion and move toward rather than away from one another in crisis.

* Help each other grow and support each other.

It's easy to see how thinking of your organization as a family unit, characterized by these traits, inherently establishes an undercurrent of caring. It's equally easy to imagine what kind of meaning and fulfillment this type of culture would foster and what kind of dedicated performance would follow suit.

Mark Bissell knows a thing or two about the power of running a business like it was family. For Mark, it is family. Mark is the CEO and namesake of Bissell, a cleaning products giant established in 1876 that is still family owned. Mark's great-grandmother, Anna Bissell, took over the business in 1889 when her husband and company founder, Melvin Bissell, died, thus becoming the first female CEO in the United States. Anna, beloved by all, put in place benefits and unemployment insurance long before the company was required to do so. She began a legacy of caring for employees like they all were family members, something Mark treasures to this day and works to carry forward.

Bissell told me:

> I truly believe the family business approach inherent in our culture is a key driver of our performance and is a competitive advantage. I view my legacy as perpetuating that strong family business culture—a culture where loyalty, honesty, and respect pays serious dividends in terms of the relationships built and the results achieved. And finding the right people to bring in and carry on the culture is even more critical for Bissell than at most other companies, because the family-oriented aspect I'm trying to preserve is such a meaningful differentiator.

Bissell went on to tell me that it's an aspect he holds above all else: "I simply won't tolerate anyone that tries to put themselves above other Bissell employees—their 'family,' so to speak."

Bissell is ahead of the game in ensuring that only the best family dynamics play out in the Bissell workplace. But that's not the case in every workplace. As you, the meaning-making manager, strive to embed family values into your own culture, it's important to be mindful of darker family theatrics that all too often play out at work. Research in workplace dynamics indeed confirms that people tend to re-create their own family dramas at the office. Do any of these situations seem familiar?

* Employees make over-the-top or desperate plays for approval from their bosses.

* They engage in backstabbing and bickering with scene-stealing coworkers.

* They bicker in meetings like at the family dinner table.

* They shy away from authority figures.

* They harbor petty jealousies toward coworkers.

* They make hypercritical judgments of subordinates or coworkers.[5]

Group dynamic researchers say the parallel should make intuitive sense considering that the first organization people ever belong to is their families, with parents the first bosses and siblings the first colleagues. "Our original notions of an institution, of an authority structure, of power and influence are all forged in the family," said Warren Bennis, the late management guru.[6]

The key is to bring all the best of a caring, family mindset to an organizational culture and leave behind all the subconsciously engrained worst aspects. A failure to do so can lead to a substantive productivity drain. A two-year study by Seattle psychologist Brian Des-Roches found that "family conflict"–type dramas routinely waste 20 percent to 50 percent of workers' time.[7]

How might your behaviors change if you acted as if your coworkers were actually family? Would you exhibit the powerful "happy family" behaviors? It's a filter that can drastically change your day-to-day interactions with others and maximize meaning derived from your relationships in the process. It can also create loyalty and a sense of connection beyond belief.

Take the astounding case of Market Basket, a seventy-one-store, 25,000-employee grocery chain based in Tewksbury, Massachusetts. The chain's workers went on a highly publicized strike, staged protests, organized a boycott, and blatantly jeopardized their jobs to force the reinstatement of their beloved CEO, Arthur T. Demoulas (affection-ately known as "Artie"). Demoulas was forced out by a rival member within his own feuding family. Even as Demoulas was embroiled in his own family's feud over the years, he continued feeding a rare company culture of which he was the heart and soul—a culture mirroring a true family environment.

Steve Paulenka, one of eight managers fired for their participation in protests, spoke of the care and concern Demoulas showed for his autistic son, Joe, after the boy suffered an accident requiring recon-structive surgery. For weeks after the accident, Demoulas inquired about Paulenka's son, never once inquiring about business matters, only asking about the well-being of the boy. The story is thematic of the kindness Demoulas regularly exhibited in an effort to treat everyone as family.

A management professor from the Massachusetts Institute of Technology who visited the picket lines found that many Market Bas-ket employees spoke of their fear that "without Artie, we won't be able to hold onto our values and we will fall into a vicious cycle."[8] Many of the employees saw it as black and white; the sense of family that Demoulas created was simply not something they could do without—they'd rather put their high-paying jobs at severe risk (Market Basket is also known for its generous pay). Sixty-eight of Market Basket's seventy-one store managers signed a petition stating they would not work for anyone other than Arthur T. Demoulas (the other three man-agers were on vacation and presumably signed the petition later).

Undaunted, Market Basket executives made it clear they would start hiring replacement workers. Equally undaunted, consumers left Market Basket in droves in support of the employees' plight (despite their love of the chain and its low prices), an abandonment that deeply threatened the very sustainability of the grocery chain itself.[9]

The unprecedented support for the beloved leader proved too strong—the board of directors caved in to a proposed buyout led by Demoulas himself, and he was reinstated as CEO.

In an age where it's hard to fathom employees putting their jobs on the line in support of a CEO, this story stands as a monument to the power of meaning-making. Labor experts have been astonished that Market Basket employees, nonunionized ones at that, would go as far as clearly risking their livelihoods to put a beloved boss back in command; such behavior has simply not been seen before. It highlights the extraordinary power a manager can have by creating a family-like, meaning-rich environment.

And it begs an interesting question.

If you were fired, who would protest or put their job at risk on your behalf?

If you are unsatisfied with the answer to this question, it's not too late or too insurmountable to change the narrative. It requires making an overt commitment to people as an organizational priority and embedding this genuine desire in the culture. It requires maintaining a tight-knit versus an arm's-length mindset, the core of the first component for building a caring culture.

Rewards and Recognition Done Right

To reward and recognize someone is perhaps the most pure and visible form of caring for and valuing another human being. The performance impacts of this Component of Caring range from increased individual productivity to increased loyalty. For example, research has shown that companies scoring in the top 20 percent for building a recognition-rich culture actually had 31 percent lower voluntary turnover rates.[10]

In general, rewards and recognition (R&R) can take many forms, both formal and informal, daily or event driven, individual or group oriented. A great R&R culture taps into all of them. In general, only the imagination limits the number of ways to recognize and reward someone.

But not all forms of R&R are created equal.

In actuality, as human beings we aren't profoundly motivated by the tangible reward or recognition itself. It's about the meaning behind the reward. In fact, an international employee survey found that almost

60 percent of the most meaningful recognition is *free*. Employees are looking for meaning, not things.[11]

And that is the distinction I make about rewards and recognition programs that are "done right." It is all too easy to drain the meaning out of R&R and miss the opportunity to create fulfillment and further inspire elevated contributions. So here are five principles to help you execute rewards and recognition in a manner that will matter.

1. *Personalize so that you don't trivialize.* A cookie-cutter approach to R&R can make recipients feel as unappreciated as if they weren't getting rewarded or recognized. Great managers take the time to understand how each employee likes to be recognized and what makes each individual employee feel valued. You can start by asking your employees:

* How do you like to be recognized? (e.g., formally or informally, in private or in public, as an individual or as part of a group, from a one-up manager/two-up manager/peer/direct report, verbally or in print)

* What form do you like the reward to take? (e.g., words of appreciation, increased responsibility, salary increase, more autonomy, challenging new work, opportunity to showcase good work, time off, being leveraged as an expert, promotion, celebration events)

Take the time to ask. You might even share your own preferences. Flesh out the many forms that rewards can take. Discuss similarities, differences, and new insights gained about each other. Identify specifically what you and your employee can do to fully value each other.

2. *Get everyone in on the act.* Managers don't have to be the only ones handing out R&R. Encourage employees to practice peer-to-peer recognition and you will create a virtuous circle of meaning.

The Oscars are the most meaningful of all awards to actors, actresses, and directors because it is an award determined by their peers—it truly is "an honor just to be nominated."[12] Appreciation from peers engenders goodwill among team members, inspires them to pay it forward, and elevates outcomes. Gallup studies indicate that when employees feel affiliation with one another, they are more likely to put in the extra effort to produce at even higher levels for their company. [13]

The good news is that stimulating such powerful recognition can be relatively simple. When you catch people in the act of recognizing someone else, let them know how much you appreciate it—reward rewarding. Remind people of the pay-it-forward effect their efforts will have. Provide simple recognition resources like thank-you cards or low-budget themed rewards. Visibly place the thank-you cards in displays in the hallway and call these areas "Appreciation Stations" to further signify the importance of R&R to the culture. The important thing is choosing to add peer-to-peer recognition to your options for rewarding and recognizing.

3. *Be frequent, but not frivolous.* Odds are you will never hear people complaining that they are receiving too much recognition. And interestingly enough, the best workers who get the most praise are often the most insecure—it's what drives them to perform (so don't assume they are being overrecognized). For anyone, missed opportunities to reward and recognize are missed opportunities to energize. However, remember that frequent, not frivolous, is the goal. Be clear about establishing what the important things are to reward and recognize (for the business and cultural mission). Whether it's leadership, risk taking, collaboration, or any other important behavior/accomplishment, clarify the kinds of behaviors that will be rewarded. And to maximize motivation linked to higher performance, be sure to celebrate results, not just activity.

Identify anchor events that, when recognized, would derive memorable meaning and motivation for the employee. Such events as a heartfelt celebration when an employee leaves a work group, making a fuss over a new employee's entry, or a thoughtfully executed recognition of an employee's anniversary can increase the frequency of R&R in a meaningful manner.

4. *Celebrate first downs and touchdowns.* Beyond supporting the right frequency of R&R, it is important to support the right breadth as well. When major results are achieved, there are invariably important milestones that happened along the way that enabled the major achievement. The supporting cast and results that led up to the major result should be celebrated in addition to the major result itself. In this way you maximize the number of rightful participants in the meaning-making efforts.

Brian Niccol talks of "celebrating first downs and touchdowns." Niccol, currently president of Taco Bell, ascended to this position at the fast-food behemoth at age 39. What was the key to his rocketlike trajectory? For certain it has to do with his reputation for being an innovator and change agent. For example, Niccol spearheaded the Doritos Locos Tacos and Breakfast Taco launches, the biggest, most successful new product innovations in Taco Bell history. While indeed these launches were a ginormous score, Niccol told me that many important interim steps and results (involving a variety of people) took place leading up to them. On the Doritos launch, for example, the restaurants had to be ready to receive the new product, the supply chain had to be established, and the deal had to be struck with Doritos. Niccol made certain to celebrate each of these accomplishments and, in the process, engendered goodwill among the breadth of troops, generated pride among employees in being part of a culture of innovation, and further inspired the kind of performance that got him to where he is today.

While I can't guarantee your trajectory will match Niccol's experience, if you celebrate the first downs with your organization, I can assure you that you'll have many meaning-making touchdowns.

5. *Deliberate the delivery.* How you deliver rewards and recognition to employees can stick the landing or crash the landing. Don't kill the intent. You should think through the delivery with attention to detail. For example, sincerity is key; if it comes from the heart it sticks in the mind.

One manager particularly skilled at delivering R&R in a meaningful manner shared her two keys to success with me: "Specificity is a must; general praise leads to a general malaise," she said. "And timeliness is critical. Drift creates a rift." Let R&R drift past the time a praiseworthy event occurred and you create a rift between receipt of the recognition and any potential for associated meaning.

Finally, you should start from a core of a strong relationship with the recipient if at all possible; otherwise rewards and recognition from you won't matter much.

Respect

Every day we have so many opportunities to recognize and value other human beings just by the way we interact with them. Think about the inverse of this statement for a moment. How many times have you unintentionally engaged in behaviors that said, "You're not worthy of my time and attention" or "You aren't important to me"? Think about the times when you are late, yet again, for a meeting. Or you don't say "hi" to people in the hallways. Or you glance at your watch when someone is talking, don't make eye contact, or are tapping away at your handheld device. Or you allow others to interrupt a conversation.

Some of the most vital opportunities for recognizing and rewarding other people are grounded in everyday common decency and respect for others, but according to the University of Michigan's Jane Dutton, *90 percent* of workers polled said workplace incivility is a problem. And this means an unnecessary barrier stands in the way of optimal performance. Dutton goes on to say: "When coworkers engage each other respectfully, they create a sense of social dignity that confirms self-worth and reaffirms competence. Respectful engagement empowers and energizes, giving individuals a heightened sense of their abilities."[14]

And the wider the net you cast to entwine people within the ropes of respect, the better.

Former President Bill Clinton once closed a speech to over 6,000 people with an exhortation to "see more people"; he was referring at the time to the volunteers behind the scenes who would clean up after the event, as an example.[15] The wisdom applies to the development of a culture of consequence, where respectful interactions and recognition of others, always and with *everyone*, is a foundational bedrock. "See more people" and you'll see more people contributing to new levels of organizational performance.

You can provide meaningful day-to-day recognition by holding sacred the act of being respectful in your interactions with others. I like to call this kind of quality human connection "respectcognition." The respectcognition you bestow on others can become a habit with some self-realization and practice. The following list is meant to serve as a "thou shalt" reminder for delivering respectful recognition.

❏ *Inquiring and listening, really listening, is recognition.* You are fundamentally recognizing an individual's worth when you really listen to the other person. Live and listen attentively in the moment. Paraphrase the main points to show you are listening. Practice the WAIT principle and ask yourself, "Why Am I Talking?" And make it a point to remember a person's name when you are newly introduced. Ever forget that person's name immediately after the fact? We can all do better.

❏ *Staying available and approachable is recognition.* You are recognizing that the opportunity to connect with you is valued and even seen as a reward. And it's okay to be professional *and* personable.

❏ *Recognizing people's state of mind is recognition.* Imagine an invisible sign around someone's neck that speaks to his or her state of mind. What does it say? Being sensitive to what may be going on in other people's lives is recognition that you care.

❏ *Recognizing different styles of communication is recognition.* Shift gears. Adjust, accommodate, appreciate. Reward people for being who they are.

❏ *Recognizing the value of others' opinions and ideas is recognition.* Seeking out opinion and input from other people, even from those not ordinarily in the loop, says, "You matter."

❏ *Constructive feedback done right is recognition.* You are recognizing (and feeding) other people's desire to grow. You are rewarding them with the investment of your time.

❏ *Recognizing the value of others' time is recognition.* Be on time yourself. Let it be known why it's important.

❏ *Recognizing the effort people put into big meetings is recognition.* They rehearse and stress the night before. They might buy new outfits. Reward them by putting them at ease. Afterward, recognize their effort.

❏ *Recognizing social comfort zones is recognition.* Use humor, but never cruel humor that comes at the cost of another human being. Reward by being fun around others, not making hurtful fun of others.

❏ *Recognizing the past is recognition.* Show respect for who worked on what, especially if you are changing a decision or direction or commenting on days gone by.

❏ *Recognizing others' existence is recognition.* Say hello to everyone you pass in the halls. No one has actually invented invisibility yet. The more names you learn and use, the better.

Work-Life Harmony

Understanding this Component of Caring requires first understanding a harsh reality—the term *work-life balance* is no longer appropriate for the modern workplace. It suggests work and life are not as intertwined as they are, thanks to email, international communications, and heavier workloads. It implies the two strands could be separated as easily as a closing whistle once ended a factory worker's shift. And no two people define "balance" the same way, which stultifies the cookie-cutter measures often used to address the issue.

The term *work-life harmony* is more indicative of what to aim for—integrating work and life harmoniously in a mutually supportive fashion that yields a net pleasing effect on the whole. After all, we only have one life, and work is a part of it, so harmony among the two is undeniably worth the pursuit. Seventy-two percent of the highly engaged agree with the statement "My organization makes it possible to balance work and personal life," which garners only 20 percent agreement among the disengaged.[16]

I've created a mnemonic—SPECIFIC—that pinpoints what you can do as a manager to help others (and yourself) make progress toward achieving work-life harmony. It involves being intentional, holistic, and specific in your approach through:

Simplification
Productivity self-audits
Energy-renewing activities
Choices
In-touch with others' situations
Flexibility
Involving others
Commit

Simplification: All in all, work-life harmony requires you to simply get serious about simplification. We often don't notice the cumulative effect of each little activity we engage in or take on until we look up and suddenly things at work seem way too complex, overwrought, and unproductive. Stop to ask, "Why are we doing what we're doing?" and "Is it worth it?" Use power questions to challenge the status quo of activity. For example, one team I worked with encouraged everyone in the organization to ask one question whenever any new work was about to be created: *Is the juice worth the squeeze?* It forces you to stop and think about what's being asked to be done and whether it's worthy of the added complexity and effort it's about to bring.[17] You can also ask: *How about half-time?* Encourage employees to hold meetings in half the time, which forces discipline and gives time back. Note that this technique is not meant to turn each meeting into a robotic drill bereft of any human connection, laughter, or fun. The point isn't to take the humanity out of the meetings, but to make the meetings more humane.

In addition to using power questions, you can employ power tools such as Save-A-Day programs, No Meeting Fridays, Shameless Reapplication (encourage people to share and/or reapply good work to avoid reinventing the wheel), and To Don't lists to drive awareness of things that tend to be low-value time wasters.

Productivity self-audits: This practice requires a self-critical lens and watchful eye to pinpoint unproductive behaviors that drain time and energy. These behaviors/bad habits must go.

Energy-renewing activities: Encourage participation in activities that will restore people's energy, so they have plenty of it when work starts *and* ends. Author Matthew Kelly takes it further when he says: "Nothing affects personal and professional satisfaction like your energy level—there is no substitute for personal energy."[18] The options for creating energy-building activities at work are endless. Create a Down the Drain program built around emphatically eliminating that drained feeling employees can get when they leave work at the end of the day. The program could encourage a healthy lifestyle and might include a voluntary weight-loss challenge. Hold an awards banquet offsite at a fun location to get everyone pumped up and energized about their accomplishments and what lies ahead. Facilitate continual learning and growth as a source of energy. Be aware of what things at work suck the life out of you and then alter your interplay with these occasions— and encourage others to do the same. Of course get the sleep, exercise, and nutrition your body needs. And make your personal well-being a priority. This is something we'll cover in the final Component of Caring.

Choices: Making choices and helping others make them is the most fundamental element of achieving work-life harmony. We instinctively know it, yet we don't do enough of it. Choices must be made based on reflection and the realization of what kind of life you want to lead and what's most important to you. Choices are not just about saying no; they are about knowing what to say no to, as part of a bigger integrated plan, then weaving all one's choices into one tapestry—one harmonious life—with work integrated accordingly. As an example, I find it vitally important to live every day trying to inspire people and/or make a difference in their lives. I have found ways to weave that driving force in my life into work, as I mentioned in Chapter 5. I regularly give key-note speeches at a variety of occasions within my own company and at other companies in pursuit of this inner need. Preparing for these occasions takes time, and I've made choices to forego a few other me-time activities that are less important so that I don't have to sacrifice family time at home. I'm trying to live one life, with work and life in harmony and mutually supportive of each other.

As a meaning-making manager, you can help your employees find work-life harmony by first helping them identify their purpose and desired legacy (from Chapters 3 and 4). Then, encourage them to prioritize what they spend their time on, feeding off their purpose and desired legacy for guidance. Guide them toward building a creative plan that helps them live one integrated life in service of what's most important to them.

In-touch with others' situations: Having manager/employee discussions about work-life harmony is critical. Get in tune with what might be hindering or helping the cause for your employee. It is then necessary to be prepared to make reasonable adjustments to job requirements or deliverables to help lessen the strain. Being creative in crafting mutually acceptable approaches to how the work gets done is also important.

Flexibility: One of the best methods for assisting work-life harmony I've encountered is the commitment to flexible work arrangements. Compressed workweeks, flex hours, less than full-time options, work-from-home schedules, and location-free jobs are just a few such examples. With all these options, it's important to be mindful of creating the right equilibrium between providing flexibility in work arrangements and keeping a sense of community and accessibility (remote workers can admittedly provide a challenge in this capacity). Provision of flexibility accompanied with accountability for delivering results also must be firmly in place. Of note, it's particularly powerful when a leader role-models a flexible work arrangement. Technology and having a base of trust between the manager and the employee are other enablers of flexibility as well.

Involve others: Working toward work-life harmony is a Herculean task; it will undoubtedly take help from others. The family should be enrolled. Coworkers can help by not scheduling meetings at the start or end of business. They can help by respecting that a one-hour meeting starting at 9 a.m. needs to end at 10 a.m., not 10:15, which can throw someone's whole day off and affect work departure time. The point is to bravely go public with the goal of work-life harmony and enlist all the help possible.

Commit: To have success in striving toward work-life harmony requires real commitment. It has to truly become a priority because there is perhaps no other goal that will inherently have more barriers.

Personal Well-Being

You care about your family members' personal well-being, their general physical health and wellness. Are they living a healthy lifestyle, getting enough exercise and sleep, eating properly, managing stress levels, and generally taking good care of themselves?

Why shouldn't these same questions be of concern to you for your work family? That's why personal well-being is the next (and final) Component of Caring.

The problem is that it is not apparent to today's workers that their managers really do care about their well-being. A global study on employee engagement showed that only 42 percent of senior leaders are seen as being supportive of policies that promote employee well-being. The impact on performance of this lack of visible leadership support is evidenced by the fact that among the highly engaged, 68 percent felt leaders supported such policies while among the disengaged only 16 percent agreed.[19] A failure by leaders to demonstrate concern for well-being practices at work is most certainly an opportunity missed.

Of course it's not difficult to imagine the positive effect that good employee health has on work productivity. Plenty of studies prove that point. The untapped potential is for managers to be thoughtful enough to *visibly show* a personal level of genuine concern for their employees' personal well-being. In fact, being well-versed in the well-being of others pumps up their sense of feeling valued.

I'm not talking about being intrusive here. Physical health and wellness is obviously a very personal issue for most people. The idea is to put effort into showing you care in approachable, low-touch ways. The very act of showing you care about something so personal to your employees as their well-being, and doing that in the right ways, can *swell* their sense of self-worth, value, and feeling cared for. I call this contributing to an employee's "swell-being."

Swell-being exists at the intersection of two essentials—core behaviors for helping people focus on well-being, and how you deliver that help, which can serve as an inflationary device to pump up an employee's sense of feeling valued and cared for (yielding swell-being). Let's talk about these core helping behaviors and how to deliver them.

❏ *Inquire about people's well-being.* Make your inquiry all about them personally, in a way that detaches from work outcomes. Tie the inquiry to thoughtful knowledge you've acquired about the person as a whole. Listen for cues that give you a natural entry into the discussion, such as when an employee says she is stressed out or can't get to exercise, for example.

❏ *Role-model healthy behaviors.* This helping behavior is delivered by looking for ways to gently get others involved in healthy behaviors you visibly role-model. For example, leave work at a reasonable hour; and as you are walking out for the day, encourage others to pack up and leave with you. Offer to move an 8:00 a.m. meeting to 8:30 a.m. so your employees can get a little more rest if they've been putting in late nights. Put vacation on a pedestal and take the time off from work that you are entitled to—work won't go off the rails without you. Surprisingly, more than 50 percent of all Americans do not take all of their vacation days and 30 percent use less than half their allotted vacation time. And yet engagement and productivity hover near all-time lows![20] Further send the message that vacation is important by talking about yours, asking about theirs, and truly unplugging and not communicating with your employees during your own vacation (or theirs). Let them know you want your vacation absence to be as valuable for them as it is for you.

❏ *Encourage involvement in healthy activities and wellness initiatives.* The method of delivery is especially important here. As you develop any wellness initiative, make participation low pressure. Incorporate employee ideas into the wellness initiative to encourage involvement and get their buy-in to a visible agenda of caring.

❏ *Help reduce stress (not cause more).* Deliver this helping behavior by learning what stresses your employees out, and then avoid these actions. Let them know you are working on it. Have fun and be fun. Be inclusive. Seek out ways to show employees you enjoy their company and having fun with them. One of my favorite sayings of all time is a quote by Victor Borge: "The shortest distance between two people is laughter."[21]

❏ *Promote work-life harmony.* Help your employees develop a SPECIFIC plan, as outlined previously.

To show you care for someone is to show that the person matters to you, which begets meaning for the recipient. This sense of meaning will lead to deeper fulfillment and higher levels of sustained performance over time. After all, don't we all want to produce for those who have shown they care about us? Now think of the other side of the coin. How hard would you work for those you know either don't care or seem indifferent about the whole you? Being mindful of and attentive to the Components of Caring will help ensure that energy-sustaining, not energy-draining, messages are sent and received.

AUTHENTICITY

Sean "Puffy" Combs was nervous. The rap icon, media mogul, and wildly successful entrepreneur was sweating and stammering, in fact. The man known in pop culture simply as "Puff Daddy" sat uncomfortably in a comfortable chair in front of over 700 marketers, while a moderator asked questions about his empire, his brand, and his plans for Revolt (his video music channel). For over fifteen minutes Combs fidgeted in his chair, rubbed his palms on his high-end business suit, and generally looked like a fish out of water. The audience sensed it and was clearly having trouble connecting with the superstar. There was a palpable sense of discomfort and unease in the air.

It was at that point that Combs leaned forward in his chair, looked out at the audience, and in a heartfelt confession said, "Look, I have to admit something to you all. This is not what I'm used to doing. Give me a microphone and 100,000 people to perform in front of and I'm fine, but this, right here and right now, just isn't natural for me." He then stood up, walked around, took a few deep breaths, and stretched—all to great applause. Then he sat back down in his chair, looking much more relaxed, composed, and relieved.

With the flip of a switch, Sean Combs opened himself up to his audience, was shockingly honest and vulnerable, and suddenly had the rapt attention of everyone. He had connected in a way that no story of self-made success or behind-the-scenes telltale could ever do.

That is the power of authenticity.

Authentic behavior binds human beings to one another, and it is deeply satisfying for those conducting and receiving; it helps reinforce self-identities and creates bridges to a sense of belonging.

In fact, as human beings, one of the most essential ways we search for meaning is by seeking to answer such fundamentally introspective questions as "Who am I?" and "Where do I belong?"[22] Along the way in the journey of our working life, we continually compare and contrast our present situations to our beliefs about who we are and where we belong. We are looking for matches and misalignments with our self-evaluations. We ask ourselves if we are fully expressing who we can be. We wonder if we are behaving genuinely and if we are in the presence of genuine others. We seek certainty of internal congruence—in ourselves and in others. When we find it, we find meaning.

As for the alternative, it is very difficult to find meaning and make sense of the working world when we are laboring in conditions that force internally disharmonious actions, create false fronts, or tolerate disingenuous behavior. As managers and workers we can promote feelings of authenticity in the workplace in three basic ways: (1) being where you belong, (2) being true to yourself, and (3) conducting yourself in an authentic manner.

Being Where You Belong

Do you feel at home at work? Does what you do for your job match up with your skills, interests, and passions? How would your employees answer this question? As managers, we have to make sure people fit their job and the organization and, just as important, make sure the organization and job are a good fit for them. We can start by ensuring that people are set up to succeed in their roles and that their roles also speak to their talents and passions. University of Michigan's Brent Rosso and fellow researchers have found that when people are intrinsically engaged by their work, when they truly enjoy it and are immersed in it, the work experience allows for expression of their authentic self.[23] By default, then, when people aren't intrinsically engaged by their work, they feel inauthentic.

If employees aren't operating with passion, aren't succeeding, or aren't a good fit, it may be time for a tough but liberating discussion. Some of the most heartfelt thank-yous that I've ever received came from employees who needed my help finding a better personal path than the one they were on. In every case, they knew deep in their heart they were struggling on some level. And while the discussions were never easy, each person was greatly appreciative of the nudge when all was said and done.

This isn't about refusing to stretch talents and encourage growth. Nor is it about yanking people from a role at the first sign of a struggle.

Rather, this is about ensuring that no one in the organization toils in a role where she feels she doesn't belong, doesn't want to belong, or can't succeed. Likewise, it's about ensuring that those who are successful at their jobs don't also feel like frauds because they aren't being successful at being themselves. The presence of any of these internal conflicts makes it difficult for us to enact the person we are meant to be. If your employees are thinking within the context of their work role, "This isn't who I am," "This isn't where I belong," or "I can't succeed here," then a dearth of meaning and a fall in performance are sure to follow.

How do you find out if someone feels at home or at sea?

Ask.

And if you've built a great, caring relationship with that person, he'll tell you.

Being True to Yourself

We've already established that meaning-rich cultures are ripe with rituals of coworkers caring for and staying true to one another. Perhaps even more important, however, is an atmosphere that encourages you to first stay true to yourself. When we have a sense of our directional DNA—our values and beliefs—and act in a manner consistent with these DNA strands, it produces a deep sense of meaningfulness.

The University of Michigan's Rosso has indeed found that at work, when people believe they are behaving consistently with their beliefs, values, and interests, it promotes feelings of a deep and authentic connection to oneself—an internal consistency.[24] This internal congruency generates a sense that we are being who we were meant to be. It helps us to make sense of the world and our place in it. We feel genuine. We feel real. We find meaning in situations and people that are real. When we are in a place where we can be ourselves and show our humanity, and when we are around others who do the same, it creates genuine connections. Authenticity means not only being true to yourself, but being able to share your true self with others. Work is a vehicle through which we can share our unique talents, creativity, and creations. Furthermore, when we can express ourselves and share our unique talents and creativity, we are able to give a gift to others and make an imprint. We are also giving ourselves the gift of energetic self-expression, which is nourishing and reenergizing and reaffirms our identity. It is meaning constructed via the materialization of our true selves.

Diane Dietz, the Safeway chief marketing officer you met in Chapter 5, is a person incapable of being anything other than exactly who she is. As she so eloquently told me, "The only one good at being someone else is an actor." And helping others be true to themselves further fuels performance because no energy is wasted on pretending.

One of the most powerful things you can do on the authenticity front is to role-model what it looks like to bring your true self to light each and every day. Be true to beget true. Truth builds trust, and trust builds bonds. Bonds allow us to accomplish much more, with much more impact.

Conducting Yourself in an Authentic Manner

Authentic behavior in and of itself is critical not only for maximizing meaning, but also for engaging and energizing people. Let's turn for a moment to perhaps the most challenging of all battlegrounds for maintaining attention and engagement—teenagers in a classroom.

Sam Intrator is a teaching expert who spent 130 days shadowing and closely observing teenagers in a diverse California high school. He discovered the key to holding their attention, making personal connections, and thus making learning meaningful for them. Is it a boisterous presentation? Is it a commanding and even fear-inducing presence? Is it a comedic or hip approach?

Nope. It's authenticity.

Intrator says, "Teachers who connected with students told poignant personal stories, conveyed their passions, and expressed emotion and vulnerability. Time and again, I heard students say about teachers who were capable of snaring attention, 'Mr. X is a real person.'"[25]

In the workplace, too, it is the existence of a real environment and accompanying genuine behavior that maximizes the quality of connections between coworkers, fires up engagement, and creates enduring moments of meaning. It starts with the primary teachers in an organization, its leaders and managers, who must role-model authentic behavior. It's easy to understand the importance of this when you imagine what it's like in an inauthentic environment where disingenuous, untrustworthy, or fake behavior is the norm. The unhealthy roots of such inauthentic behavior will soon kill the tree that's trying to grow. Moreover, the offending acts don't remain buried; disingenuous behavior has a way of surfacing and revealing itself. Human instinct is strong and in tune to a lack of authenticity.

In fact, nothing is more transparent than when someone's not being transparent.

And again, the effects can be devastating.

Think of the incredibly negative emotions you have toward people when they are not being transparent and you know it. It's hard to repair. Now think of how energizing it is when you are encountering someone being genuine and honest. Why wouldn't you always seek to create that kind of energy? The truth is, most managers absolutely want to be transparent and authentic. However, the problem arises in the level of vigilance required. Well-meaning managers can ruin years of goodwill with just one unintentional slip.

Adhering to a code of conduct for authenticity is one helpful way to ensure the right behaviors are always top of mind. Sharing these principles with your organization can help set behavioral expectations and standards. Accordingly, I've outlined a code of conduct for being authentic.

Be a Beacon of:

 ✳   Transparency, honesty, and integrity

Be Worthy of:

 ✳   Belief and trust

Behave:

 ✳   In a genuine, down-to-earth, and approachable manner (no matter the conditions)

* In a manner congruent with your values and character (at work and outside of work)

* With humility, humanity, and vulnerability

* Without regard to position-power, leveraging relationship-power instead

Believe:

* In the power of each person bringing his or her whole self to work, and encourage individuals to bring forth their unique skills, styles, and original thinking

Be Beholden to:

* Employees who speak truth, expose issues, and admit mistakes (and do so yourself)

Be the First to:

* Live the values of the organization (especially if you establish them)

* Show passion and productive emotion

* Give credit away and accept blame

* Laugh, have fun, and encourage others to do the same

Be Wary of:

* Politics and two-faced behavior

Be a Provider of:

* Truth, reality, and hope

* Genuine feedback that is positive and corrective (and from the heart)

* A safe haven for taking risks and venting frustrations

All in all, promoting an atmosphere of authenticity and creating caring environments help yield norms of behavior that forge strong, meaningful bonds and produce vastly stronger results. But to maximize the amount of meaning for employees and heighten their performance, it requires going beyond mere interconnectedness to interdependence. This leads us to the third element of the most meaning-rich cultures.

TEAMWORK

Individual fulfillment is often a joint effort. Let's now look at the primary manners in which teamwork makes meaning and fosters sustained elevated performance along the way.

Teamwork Engenders Esprit de Corps

Teamwork creates a sense of pride, fellowship, camaraderie, and loyalty. Research shows that being cared about by teammates is a strong predictor of engagement as well.[26] Furthermore, teamwork enables relationships to form and accordingly nurtures a sense of connectedness and belongingness. It serves as a source of answers to the self-reflective question, Where do I belong?[27] I've seen many examples of teams crystallizing this sense of belonging in the form of metaphors used to brand the team and create a common identity (metaphors like an Everest mountain-climbing team, a village, a tribe, a family business, an incorporated business, NASA mission control, and even a family crest that challenged each team member to uphold the "family honor"). Social psychologists Michael Hogg and Deborah Terry give credence to this behavior in pointing out that "membership in workplace groups drives meaning through a sense of shared identities, beliefs, or attributes and because team members feel like they belong to something special."[28]

Teamwork Enables Interdependence

The key to creating something special and something maximally meaningful within teams is to skillfully move even further beyond a feeling of esprit de corps and interconnectedness to interdependence.

Social psychologists Shinobu Kitayama and Hazel Rose Markus take it further in stating that "greater interdependence is more meaningful for people than the pursuit of individual goals."[29] Indeed, meaning is not just derived from how individuals relate to their work, but also from how individuals relate to each other. When they relate in a manner that belies a true sense of dependency on one another, it leads to the creation of something special.

If I were to ask you to imagine a special workplace teeming with teamwork as well as authenticity and its own brand of caring, what would jump to mind?

Would it be a *steel mill*?

Probably not. But these cultural elements are palpable at Worthington Industries, a stalwart steel manufacturer and one of the original U.S. companies that cared enough for its employees to institute profit sharing. Worthington has survived and thrived through the leanest of years in this tough industry due in no small part to its culture of intense interdependence.

It is this sense of interdependence that produces meaning, and that produces. Worthington has been recognized as one of the "best thirty performing stocks in the last thirty years" and heralded in a variety of Best Companies to Work For lists.[30] Greg Ames, director of new product development, describes Worthington's culture as one of authenticity, "where the stripes come off when problems arise." He indicates it is also a culture of interdependence and mutual accountability where the core motivation is the fact that it's a lean organization where everyone has a job to do and "someone else is counting on you."

Oh, and one other fact—it's a workplace that handles tons of metal and fire in high-speed manufacturing.

So mutual accountability, which stems from a need for safety, takes on a whole other level of importance when lives depend on it. Ames says:

Mutual accountability is one of the most powerful forces on earth and it leads to a tremendous amount of teamwork and a supreme level of performance. And the performance sustains because it means something to know that you really matter to someone else's ability to do their job. It's both rewarding and a responsibility.

The culture of caring and interdependence permeates the company. Some of the company's lore revolves around stories. Like the one about one of the company presidents getting up early to shovel the walks so that none of the 8,000 employees would have to trudge through the slippery slush and risk getting hurt.

While most of us may not work in workplaces where interdependence is so central because it can literally save lives, what would happen if we acted like it did? There are lessons and inspiration to be taken from the power of the culture at companies such as Worthington.

Similarly, there is a lot at stake behind the work at Cincinnati Children's Hospital Medical Center, rated number three among children's hospitals in the nation and among the top ten in all ten specialties ranked by *U.S. News & World Report*. CEO Michael Fisher was quick to share with me what he feels is the driving force behind the hospital's elevated performance and national recognition.

A sense of interdependence.

The field of patient care is one inherently rich in meaning. It naturally draws people who are seeking to make a measurable, visible difference in the lives of others. But at Cincinnati Children's, the leadership team also draws meaningfulness from the relationships and sense of interdependence they've forged with one another. They are united in their deep sense of mutual dependence to deliver on the hospital's meaningful vision to be the leader in improving child health. This sharp sense of interdependence has allowed Cincinnati Children's to separate itself from the pack, a sense that starts with Fisher himself. Fisher says:

There are three planks I oversee: clinical care, research, and training/education. I'm not a doctor, scientist, or nurse by training, so by default I can't micromanage. [That's] true, by the way, for finance or IT as well. But I do know that people value being valued, and that interdependence is an absolute requirement for us to excel, as is accountability for the whole. You have independence to run your area but have the responsibility to contribute to the success of the whole. For example, the chief of pediatrics in the research foundation needs to lead the pediatrics enterprise, but I also need him to help broadly with the overall success of the hospital's enterprise, and hold his peers accountable for great marketing or great IT. I truly believe that great organizations have a spirit of independence without the malady of autonomy: Do your thing but you are responsible for success of the whole enterprise—they are intertwined.

These stories illustrate that organizations and managers adept at fostering world-class teamwork (and the sense of meaning and fulfillment that goes with it) very intentionally drive a sense of mutual interdependence to pull a loosely connected group into a tight-knit unit.

You can facilitate the same sense of interdependency in your place of work.

Here's how.

It requires understanding the kind of team goals that foster interdependency, being attentive to the impact that team deliverables and role definitions can have on fostering a sense of interdependency, and spelling out specific expectations for interdependent behavior.

❏ *Establish 3C goals.* Interdependency starts with having goals for the team that are Common, Compelling, and Cooperative. The commonality ensures everyone is working toward the same end. The goal has to be compelling enough to create energy on its own and draw each person toward it. Furthermore, it has to be cooperative in nature—each team member must realize the goal is lofty enough that the only way the goal can be accomplished is by the team working together (versus a set of individuals working to achieve the goal in silos).

❏ *Ensure specific deliverables are in place.* Specific deliverables can be well-defined endpoints or points specified at various stages along the way that indicate a team is progressing toward its goal. These deliverables help pinpoint and guide how a team should spend its collective energy. The time-bound and measurable nature of specific deliverables further draws team members together and elevates the sense of interdependency.

❏ *Define and share each team member's role.* Specifically list the role of each team member and what strengths each brings to the table, and share it with the whole team. Role awareness drives real accountability; each team member knows what to expect from the other and how each team member fits into the equation. No one can be mentally dismissed simply because it's not understood how or what he or she contributes. An overt inventory of each person's strengths increases the likelihood that team members will call on one another in times of specific need.

❏ *Establish expectations for interdependent behavior.* These are the sacred behaviors and expectations—those that directly contribute to a sense of interdependency and the feeling that each team member is accountable to one another.

* *Commitment.* This is an absolute mandatory. Believe in the mission. Pour your hearts into it and show a passion to win. Lack of commitment from any one team member will divide a team. And when it comes to decision making along the way—debate, decide, commit. Lack of commitment to a decision is poisonous and can derail a sense of teamwork.

* *Accountability.* Raise your hand and own less-than-ideal results; point your finger and share success. Know how your performance affects "the rest of the assembly line." You are accountable to the whole. Hold others accountable for their part and expect the same.

* *Expertise.* Know, show, and share yours. Value other members' expertise and leverage it for support when needed. Interdependency blossoms when a team instinctively draws together to brainstorm solutions and tap into each other's knowledge to solve tough issues.

✳ *Attitude.* Multiply the positive. The alternative will alienate you.

✳ *Honesty.* There is no greater repellant than someone acting or speaking without honor. One discovered untruth or failure to act with openness disintegrates trust and the desire to inter- act. Integrity integrates, deception distances. Teammates must be honest with each other at all times and provide corrective feedback when necessary.

✳ *Openness.* Ask for help when needed. Ask it from each other and from up the chain. Bring up the tough issues when neces- sary and call for help. The chain of command provides strength. That's why it's not called a thread of command.

✳ *Camaraderie.* Building rapport and forming bonds with team members creates emotional accountability. When you enjoy the people you work with, you don't want to let them down. Everyone is drawn closer together and more likely to go the extra mile to help each other. Camaraderie with workmates means you want to pick them up when things are tough and you want to role-model resiliency to help them recover from setbacks. And they will return the favor.

✳ *Team-first mentality.* Virtually any member of a historically great sports team will talk about the importance of putting the team's mission before any personal goals. This mindset creates a shared sense of accountability toward something bigger than the individual. Reward individual accomplishments, but also create incentives for collaborative, team-based behavior.

To take all of this a step further, you can even put the 3C goals, deliverables, role definitions, and behavioral expectations into a ver- sion of a team charter that I call (tongue in cheek) a "Declaration of Interdependence." Such a document can provide that extra bit of disci- pline to ensure that the sense of interdependency and corresponding meaning is upheld over time.

Teamwork Creates a Shared Learning Lab

An environment rich in teamwork has the propensity to spark rich learning for each team member. A team environment where everyone is working well together serves as a shared learning lab where people are comfortably learning from one another through the sharing of experiences, wisdom, and role modeling. This unique brand of learning would not be possible if each person was working on his or her own or within a dysfunctional team. And personal learning and growth is fundamental to the derivation of greater meaning and performance. You can apply many of the principles of learning and personal growth (discovered in Chapter 5) to the team environment, helping to ensure growth is maximized in this setting as well.

Teamwork Results in Meaningful Results

Great teamwork leads to a quantity and quality of accomplishments that a collection of individuals alone simply cannot achieve. John C. Maxwell, author of *Teamwork 101*, says that "teamwork divides the effort and multiplies the effect."[31] The multitude of accomplishments achieved uniquely through great teamwork correspondingly feeds the sense that the team member is playing in a winning organization, a "culture of champions" as one manager described to me. This further drives a sense of pride in membership and a feeling of fulfillment; it's internally rewarding to be a part of a team that matters.

Furthermore, great teamwork has the kind of effect on the breadth, depth, and height of results that is worth recognizing and celebrating. Great teams producing great results make people feel as if *they matter* on a team that matters. This feeling of truly making a difference on something significant feeds into sustained heightened performance, which leads to more meaning and more fulfillment (enter the cycle of profound performance). Not surprisingly, studies show that when employees work in teams and have the trust and cooperation of their team members, they outperform individuals and teams that lack good relationships.[32]

Former CEO of Procter & Gamble and ex-chairman of Disney, John Pepper believes to his core in the power of meaning-rich teamwork to produce extraordinary results. Pepper told me about several leaders he was privileged to work with after his retirement from P&G who brought this reality to life:

> At Disney, Bob Iger, the CEO, brought dramatically strengthened teamwork and collaboration among all the business and functional heads: consumer products, film, TV, Disney Channel, games, parks, etc. It hadn't always been that way. People had tended to operate to a considerable degree in silos, like in many companies. But with Bob's strong leadership, it quickly became clear to all that, working together, there were enormous opportunities for Disney to touch millions of more consumers with far more products and experiences, with much greater commercial success. The Finding Nemo, Toy Story, and Pirates of the Caribbean franchises are great examples. From the brilliant movies which spawned these franchises flowed consumer products, mobile games, experiences in the park, digital storybooks, [and] crossruff promotions on the Disney Channel. Teamwork and creative insights on how to engage children and adults more broadly made all this possible. It was a foundation for Disney's stellar financial performance over the past several years.

Pepper also shared with me his experience with the president of Yale University, Rick Levin, with whom John served as chairman of the Yale University board and, for two years, as vice chairman of finance and administration, reporting to Rick:

> I have never seen a leader bring together and empower a team better than Rick Levin. It was truly a community, which is the most rare and difficult-to-match competitive advantage an organization can have. This sense of being a community, which flows from strong teamwork, produces fierce commitment and loyalty. I've

never heard anyone convey the power of this more compellingly than Alison Richard, who served as provost under Levin. At a press conference regarding her new role as vice-chancellor of Cambridge University, Richard said this about her time on the Yale team:

> *If there is one thing I could bring [from Yale], it would be the sense of warmth and partnership and shared purpose that I feel with my many friends and colleagues at Yale. You can have the biggest endowment in the world, and you can have the best governance system in the world, but if you don't have that sense of community, then all that is for naught. If you do have that sense of community, then the sky's the limit.*

That's what great teamwork will do. This is what I experienced during my forty-year career again and again at Procter & Gamble, when we were at our best.

Teamwork produces meaning, and meaningful results.

You can further connect the two by keeping a focus on results and by celebrating that those results—and each team member's contribution to those results—really matter.

Teamwork not only directly contributes to achieving meaningful results, it is also the most direct contributor to the ultimate cultural end-state: achieving a sense of community.

WORK IN A COMMUNITY, NOT A CORPORATION

An invigorating workplace culture is absolutely fundamental for the derivation of meaning, fulfillment, and corresponding sustained elevated performance. Building your culture on the elements of caring, authenticity, and teamwork will add up to a highly spirited workplace brimming with positive attitude, energy, determination, and a deep sense of connectedness. The goal is to have all the cultural underpinnings in place to help you make your company *more of a community, less of a corporation*.[33] This way you create a sense of "being in it together," which serves as a tremendous source of meaning, as Harvard professors of organizational behavior Joel Podolny and Rakesh Khurana indicate: "When our activity at work produces an acute sense of awareness of those with whom we share the same circumstances and often the same fate, we experience work as meaningful. Such an organizational setting is what organizational scholars call a natural community, a state in which self and surrounding are inseparable."[34]

When all is said and done, a culture of consequence goes well beyond window dressing to create deep connections up, down, and across an organization. It provides the foundation for an enriched community that creates a sustainable competitive advantage and delivers sustained superior performance through its highly motivated employees.

CHAPTER 8

Meaning-Making Leadership

THE LEADER'S JOB IS TO MAKE MONEY, NOT MEANING, RIGHT?

You should know the answer to this question by now.

Meaning-making might not be in the leader's job description, but it's in the job manifestation. Whether you like it or not, as a leader you live in a fishbowl where every move can add or subtract to the meaning and emotional connectedness that your employees feel.

As a meaning-making leader, think of yourself as a master electrician—you help hardwire a network of emotional connections, linking the employee to the employer and vice versa, and both to a greater good. The Markers of Meaning that I've brought to life throughout this book constitute the wiring in the workplace network. Through your conduct and communications, you can help others find meaning *in* and *at* work. You can help employees answer with satisfaction these deeply internal questions: Why am I here? What's the point? Where do I belong? Who am I?[1] As Dave and Wendy Ulrich write in *The Why of Work*, "Leaders are meaning makers: as organizations become an increasing part of the individual's sense of identity and purpose, leaders play an increasing role in helping people shape the meaning of their lives."[2]

Furthermore, not being mindful of your role in enabling meaning

175

would be akin to ignoring strategy and vision. Your meaning-making can have that level of effect on sustained performance.

In fact, as a leader you have the ability to activate all the Markers of Meaning for your employees, especially the sixth one: feeling connection with and confidence in leadership and the mission (and knowing you fit within the mission and can uniquely contribute to it).

So far this book showed how you can make meaning in the trenches. Now let's look at what you can do from higher elevation.

TRAITS OF MEANING-MAKING LEADERS

Leaders adept at meaning-making tend to have four traits that you can incorporate into your own style. They focus not on how to *do* as much as how to *be*:

1. Have a passion for potential.

2. Emit a caring, connective undercurrent.

3. Possess framing finesse.

4. Create an atmosphere of relaxed intensity.

You don't have to demonstrate all four constantly; however, as the following case studies illustrate, most leaders adept at meaning-making are strong in at least one or two of these traits, almost as their calling card. Take inspiration from the traits you find most compelling, and consider how you might emulate them in your own way.

Have a Passion for Potential

Nancy Kramer, named one of the 100 most influential women in advertising history by *Ad Age*, grew up thinking she was stupid.

When the founder and chairman of Resource (the largest independent digital agency in the country) told me her story I was flabber-gasted. Her mother and brother teased her so much about being a "dumb blonde" while growing up that she began to believe it. This experience inspired Kramer's most deeply held credo, one that underpins the value at Resource she treasures the most: "Inside every single person there is a genius."

Kramer believes that we all have negative thoughts in our heads (which she says she still deals with to this day) that keep us from reaching our fullest potential. But when these negative thoughts can be muted and the genius allowed to speak up, both student and teacher derive fulfillment. Her passion for the limitless potential in others, herself, and in her company is palpable when you hear her talk. She epitomizes this leadership trait.

Says Kramer:

> I see myself not as the sun shining down, but the soil. I'm the enabler—my job is to give the seeds the nutrients they need to grow into complex, strong trees. I really do see myself as the dirt. I'm here to help employees get what they need to grow into their full potential. And I really do believe that if you can dream it, it's possible. The bottom line is that I'm here to serve the people in the business, not the other way around.

Kramer's deeply held passion that every person should be respected and have the right to reach his or her full potential extends to gay and lesbian rights in the workplace, a subject matter for which she has testified in Congress as a nationally recognized and respected thought leader.

She is just as passionate about her own potential and that of her company. It was this focus on what's possible that led Nancy to dream and then make real the idea of the first-ever live streaming of the Victoria's Secret Fashion Show—an event that literally shut down the Internet and at the time was hailed as the marketing event of 1998. She asks that all her employees carry out, each and every day, the core value of realizing potential and believing that you can make anything possible. It's a crucial part of the culture that Kramer expects each employee to continually feed. In fact, she likens the culture at Resource to a piece of jewelry: "Like a sterling silver bracelet that can be kept shiny by the oils from our skin, our culture only becomes tarnished when you take it off and put it in the drawer." The sum total of all of this passion for potential is a highly fulfilling workplace, with Resource being recognized and called out as such on multiple Top Places to Work lists.

Leaders like Nancy inspire you to make a difference every day. They challenge and grow you in energizing ways, encourage and reassure you as you go, give autonomy, and make you believe you can accomplish anything. Combined, these emphases trigger the second, third, fourth, as well as the sixth Markers of Meaning. Accordingly, leaders with a passion for potential are ultimately rewarded with passionate performance. You can do the same for your people.

Emit a Caring, Connective Undercurrent

Linda Kaplan Thaler may be the only person on the planet to have made Bill and Hillary Clinton cry, each on separate occasions.

Such is the depth of caring and ability to connect with others that is engrained in Linda, the chair of Publicis Kaplan Thaler ad agency and coauthor of several bestselling books, including *The Power of Nice*. Kaplan Thaler was the creative lead for the biographical ad that helped launch Bill Clinton's first bid for president. Clinton's first viewing of the emotional ad about his very poor upbringing and journey to running for president brought a tear to his eye and immediately prompted him to watch the ad over and over again. Kaplan Thaler's remarkable ability to connect in an empathetic, relatable manner played out in the portrayal of Clinton's story of hope—and it struck a chord deep within Bill Clinton himself.

At a different time, when Hillary Clinton was undergoing a tumultuous run for senator, Kaplan Thaler sensed that a well-placed kind word was what Hillary needed most. So, she leaned into a bedecked Hillary's ear at a cocktail fundraiser and told her, "I know you are an amazing first lady, and you'll make a great senator, but you know what—you really are a beautiful woman." After an exchange of hugs, Clinton looked at Kaplan Thaler with tear-filled eyes and said, "Thanks. You will never know how much I needed to hear that."

Kaplan Thaler's unending compassion for others, ability to sense what they need, and skill at making personal connections makes her a prototype for the caring, connective undercurrent trait.

Robin Koval, CEO and president of Legacy (the leading nonprofit organization in youth smoking prevention and cessation)—and cofounder of the Kaplan Thaler Group, coauthor with Linda on *The Power of Nice* and other books, and Linda's sixteen-year friend—put it to me this way:

> Linda is extraordinarily empathetic, which is a vastly underrated business skill. Yes, it makes you a better friend, spouse, parent, but its impact in the workplace runs wide and deep—it touches and motivates beyond belief.
>
> Linda has an ability to sense what people need and then care enough to give it to them, which is what makes her such a great leader. And to deliver such a message with an authentic under-tone—that's so Linda. The truth is we all want to follow somebody who we think understands us and that we can connect with. And Linda cares enough to pay attention to what inspires an individual, what is magical about someone's work, even if the person doesn't see it yet. Then, because she understands where it is coming from, she helps the person take it to a place they didn't imagine they could take it to. People are almost cultish in how much they want to work for and with her; it's because she cares so much and knows how to connect with everyone in a way that helps make them better than they actually thought they were.

Both Koval and Marjorie Porter, another longtime Kaplan Thaler employee and friend, confirmed stories of extraordinary caring and connectivity. Porter notes that Linda has paid out of her own pocket on more than one occasion to help an employee in need and is always the one to remember the details when someone's child is graduating and needs x or y. Said Porter:

Whenever anyone ever has anything going on causing turmoil in their life, Linda flips a switch and turns it—how can I help you? She is extremely connected to the people she works with. If you walk in and you don't look happy she immediately asks, what's wrong? And you find yourself easily drawn into talking everyday watercooler talk with her, totally forgetting she is a high-powered exec—her authenticity and approachability runs that deep. She is honored all the time in this industry and honestly doesn't understand why. She has multiple offices in multiple locations now and is known to sit near the ladies' room in each building from time to time so she can personally catch up with as many individuals as possible—"that's where all the action is!" You absolutely believe she cares; it's a profound difference versus other leaders. She has unswerving respect for others—everyone. And it all makes you want to stretch and perform at your absolute best for her.

Mega-selling author James Patterson once asked Linda, "Do you have any female role models in your life?" Kaplan Thaler's response was: "I don't know how to answer; I don't have one." To which Patterson simply said, "No, but you are becoming one for a lot of other people."

Kaplan Thaler herself told me her desired legacy, which typifies this meaning-making leadership trait: "I just want to teach the world that you can lead with kindness," she said. "If everybody is thinking about how they can connect with and help everyone else, you can't help but flourish. I lead by sensing what others need, and then putting my head on their shoulders."

Caring, connective leaders draw people to them and draw the best out of them. They connect with others because they genuinely care about them, respect them, and wear it on their sleeves, and because they couldn't alter their truly authentic aura if they tried. Such a mixture means the fifth (and sixth) Markers of Meaning have been engaged, and that employees will stay engaged.

Possess Framing Finesse

Julien Mininberg, former CEO of Kaz (a global healthcare and home appliances business), spearheaded a dramatic turnaround for the company. He took it from the brink of insolvency to astonishing year-on-year growth, doubling its revenue and delivering five consecutive years of record profits by 2014. It later earned him the position of CEO at Helen of Troy, the consumer products parent to Kaz.

How did he and his team do it?

Mininberg delivered Kaz's redemption via a redefinition of sorts.

He has poured his heart and soul into, by his own words, "reframing what it means to come to work each and every day at the company," thus creating a highly professional and supremely motivated organization in place of a less professionally managed, family-owned business. Organizational behavior scholar Joel Podolny and his team of researchers indicate that "leaders frame the mission, goals, purpose, and identity of the organization for employees in ways that influence their perceptions of the meaning of their work."[3]

Such is the labor of love for Mininberg, who possesses great framing finesse. He puts tremendous energy and skill into deftly framing perceptions in a host of ways that fundamentally motivate and create meaning for his organization.

It starts with Mininberg's truest passion: building a fulfilling, winning culture. It's something that was specifically pinpointed in the press release announcing his ascension to CEO of Helen of Troy. The culture, values, and beliefs at Kaz, feverishly written by Mininberg in a "Jerry Maguire manifesto-like" moment during a vacation, served as a new framework that shaped and molded employee self-perception and imbued their work and career development with greater meaning. Says Mininberg:

> By making culture come to life every single day, there is a reframing of what coming to work means. It is very rewarding to have employees come up to me after a business win where we grew market share or struck a new deal with a customer, or after a holiday party in which we recognized record results and long service

records, and tell me that "the smell of the place" is a lot different now [and] much better. This kind of sentiment is built by our cultural beliefs, which literally hang on the walls of each Kaz office around the world, on huge posters the size of a set of French doors. It reframes the entire tonality at work, changing it from "I go to work, they pay me, I do the best I can," to "I own my business, this is my thing, I am here to do whatever it takes to win." It seeps into their hearts and minds and becomes part of their identity—a code to live by at work.

Mininberg worked with other leaders at the company and the board of directors to create a new global leadership team at Kaz. He put enormous focus on creating the company's first-ever strategic plan, a set of objectives, goals, strategies, and measures that he constantly referred to as a way of continually reframing discussions and decisions made. By providing the context of such a holistic plan, he helped his leadership team and the employees they managed to make sense of how things all fit together, and to excel in their efforts. Many of these people were the same ones who had been struggling to get strong results under the company's prior leadership.

His messaging in town hall meetings always includes comments that help recast the subject matter in context of how it fits into the broader mission and strategies of the company. He takes pride in the fact that Kaz has become a learning organization that sees its leaders continually trying to teach, reframe, and help employees connect the dots at opportune times.

Says Mininberg:

We spend time making sure on-the-job learning opportunities are continually taken advantage of during the business day. I go out of my way to personally tie back what we are discussing and doing to our strategic plan. I scour for teachable moments, creating what I call "the thirty-second classroom." I will literally stop a meeting and properly frame and relate the topic we are about to make a decision on to something else in the company or [outside the company that's in the news] to show its strategic relevance and consistency. I insist that our managers from the SVP level and higher do the same, helping make it a teaching and learning organization. It helps make what we are doing and deciding together more meaningful to the employees, who can then do the same in turn with their own teams.

Mininberg also personally teaches standing-room-only classes to new hires and midlevel employees that frame the kind of leadership he is looking for. All of these efforts mean Mininberg triggers the sixth Marker of Meaning, because no one is left feeling disconnected from the company's leaders or its mission, and all feel they are positioned to uniquely contribute to the mission.

Mininberg's framing finesse runs deep, and his substantive emotional intelligence certainly has been tested. He and other leaders at Kaz helped the board of directors of what at the time was a family-controlled business to make very difficult, emotional decisions—decisions such as closing all of the company's plants and moving to an outsourcing model to improve the financial performance of the company. These plants housed many longtime employees who were also longtime friends of the controlling family. The historical headquarters of the company were moved as well, to other locations that had the right combination of managers and business fundamentals to drive the turnaround. Mininberg helped frame all these tough calls in such a way that the board understood how much making the right call mattered—to the solvency of the company and to their own legacy of what they had built as a family. Of course, there was rigorous analysis behind the kinds of tough decisions the board had to make, but as Mininberg told me, "In the end it was the *emotional understanding* as much as the numbers that allowed the board to approve the actions that turned out to be key drivers of the turnaround."

This understanding was one that Mininberg compassionately elicited through finessed framing.

Mininberg and the leadership team he helped assemble make sure employees understand that their work matters every single day. He has even inspiringly reframed others' work by helping them to articulate their purpose and desired legacy (all of which helps trigger the first

Marker of Meaning). He has reframed his own work as well, role-modeling what it means to have identified one's purpose and legacy and then striving to live by it. He states his own purpose quickly and clearly as "building the business, organization, and culture to achieve a result truly earned." His desired legacy is to "create a culture of excellence and instill principles in others such that the group that follows long after I'm gone can achieve even bigger and better success."

Julien Mininberg is the kind of leader who helps connect the dots for his employees, helping them to feel confidence in and connection with the work they're doing, the place they're doing the work at, and the people they're doing the work with. Such leaders frame and mold perceptions, mold meaning, and mold winners.

And you can, too.

Create an Atmosphere of Relaxed Intensity

Linda Kaplan Thaler is the first to laugh at a joke or open a meeting with a funny story, and yet is the last to give an inch to the competition (she's been called "the fiercest competitor you'll ever meet").

Nancy Kramer laughs when I tell her she's known for creating an atmosphere of "relaxed intensity." She tells me, "Yes, that's me. The intensity comes from my push to bring out the genius, and the relaxed describes the fact that I do so with a smile and a twinkle in the eye." Julien Mininberg is passionate about taking time to laugh, and just as passionate about making competitors cry.

Leaders who excel at meaning-making also want to win, and they want to have fun while winning, so they tend to excel at creating an atmosphere of what I call "relaxed intensity." The strong desire to win fuels the sense of being on a united, winning team and imbues people's work with a greater sense of purpose. The strong desire to have spirited fun along the way further fuels motivation.

Having fun and laughing at work can change attitudes, draw people closer together, and step-change engagement levels. Using humor eases tension, helps you sell, and gets creativity flowing. In fact, Dr. David

Abramis at Cal State Long Beach has extensively studied the field of workplace fun. He's found that people who have fun on the job are not only more creative, but they are more productive, better decision makers, and get along better with coworkers as well. They also have fewer absentee, late, and sick days than people who state they aren't having fun.[4]

Working in an atmosphere of relaxed intensity enhances the feeling that you are part of something special. Externally focused competitiveness nets a greater sense of mission while shared levity yields a greater sense of camaraderie and belongingness. This combination helps employees better connect with leadership and each other. Markers of Meaning light up like the faces of joyful employees along the way.

So while you are pushing hard and heavy for great results, lighten up.

MEANING-MAKING MESSAGING

"People may not remember exactly what you did,
or what you said, but they will always remember
how you made them feel."

—MAYA ANGELOU[5]

More than one CEO has told me, "Leadership is 90 percent communication," and research bears them out by showing that the way in which managers communicate with employees is one of the most important factors in driving employee engagement.[6] The late Maya Angelou pinpoints the key to communication that engages and makes meaning: Make people *feel* something. Inspire a felt sense of confidence. Build certainty and community. It makes the difference between compliance and commitment, meaningless work and meaningful work. It triggers the sixth Marker of Meaning.

Here are five ways to ensure your messaging will truly matter.

1. *Articulate a compelling vision that resonates with people's identities.* Research shows that compelling visions make membership within an organization feel special, enriching, and meaningful in and of themselves. They also create meaning by appealing to and resonating with members' identities.[7] Identities are formed through self-definition of core values and association with the organization's values. If you make evident how the vision supports known personal and company values, you've thus reaffirmed individual and collective identities. Similarly, when you communicate the vision in a way that strengthens the sense of community, the "we're in this togetherness," it further enhances the message's meaning.

2. *Drive mission fit.* As noted in Chapter 3, mission fit can have a very positive impact on performance and meaning derived from work. If you help connect the dots by communicating how your employees' work fits into the broader mission, you enhance their feelings of self-worth and certainty. Your employees also want to understand that what they are specifically being asked to do really matters and that it is worthy of their time and energy. Addressing these basic human needs is effectively helping to answer the deeply held questions: What's the point? Where do I belong? How do I fit in?[8]

3. *Be confident when communicating.* There is an old adage in leadership that says, "An organization is never more confident than its leader." When you communicate with confidence it breeds belief and a sense of certainty. Even in the face of mistakes, your confidence should show up in the form of unswerving accountability as well as self-confidence in course correction, while excuses should be absent. As a confident leader, you can communicate hope even as you are outlining reality. You'll help create a sense of community as optimism translates into a pride of being involved in an organization with promise. Furthermore, when you communicate your confidence in the troops and their ability to carry out the mission, it nets an increase in your employees' sense of self-efficacy.

4. *Tell stories of significance.* Organizational behavior researchers Tom Lawrence and Sally Maitlis indicate that storytelling is a vital meaning-making leadership skill. You can make meaning when you share stories of "sparkling moments"—when the team really nailed it, when they overcame adversity, or when they achieved accomplishments that have been more broadly taken for granted.[9] Such stories allow the protagonists a moment in the sun and motivate others to become the protagonists of future stories. Such stories provide hope and engender resiliency.

Paul Smith, storytelling expert and author of *Lead with a Story*, says that "stories move us. They engage us. They inspire us. Stories give us examples of how to act and how not to act. The best ones stay with us forever." And if they remember your narrative, that means it mattered, which says you just created meaning.[10]

5. *Share goals with intrinsic, not just extrinsic, value.* How many times have you found yourself introduced to a big, honking goal and walked away uninspired? Odds are the goal was "for the man"—that is, to make more profit, to drive ten points more of sales, to deliver something that, in all honesty, you didn't really personally connect with.

Professor Teresa Amabile and researcher Steven Kramer of Harvard Business School discern between intrinsic and extrinsic goal types. They cite Google's inspiring stated mission to "organize the world's information and make it universally accessible and useful" and contrast it to the stated goal of a chemicals company ("launch innovative blockbusters that will yield a minimum of $100 million in revenue annually, and do so within five years").[11]

Which goal is more motivating to you? No contest.

You can make meaning when you ask yourself a few simple questions before articulating a goal to the people in your organization:

❑ What's in it for them?

❑ How will this goal connect with them personally and emotionally?

❑ How might accomplishment of this goal help them to grow, and what else might it mean to them personally if the goal is achieved?

If you communicate goals with heavy extrinsic value only, you effectively say to the people in your organization, "You need to hit this goal because it's important to my advancement," when instead you should be implicitly saying, "Here's a goal that will advance what I need, what the company needs, and what you need in order to derive a greater sense of meaning, fulfillment, and accomplishment in your work."

SPECIALTY MEANING-MAKING MESSAGING

There are crucial moments as a leader where your communications can really connect and make meaning, or really muck it up. These disproportionately important moments matter, and so should your communications in such times. For example, as a manager you have undoubtedly experienced the angst that comes with starting a new job and working with a new organization or team. Will I succeed? Will they like me? Will we connect?

Now imagine what your new organization must be thinking when you arrive—and what you likely thought when you got a new manager yourself. Angst times ten. What are your hot buttons? What's important to you? What is your agenda? Will the new manager like me?

And with this angst comes perhaps the most personal question of all that employees will subconsciously ask themselves: What will this new leader mean *for* me, and *to* me?

What an opportunity to make a meaningful connection.

You can dispel all the mystery by publicly declaring the few simple things that serve as your guiding principles. People are trying to read you, anyway; why not open the book for them?

I have an exercise in transparency to share with you: my own set of beliefs spelled out, which I've shared with various organizations over the years. They've let organizations get to know me, eased their fears, and jump-started our relationships. All the faster to gain the troops' confidence and bolster their confidence in themselves.

MY OPEN BOOK BELIEFS

✳ ✳ ✳

Over time and through introspection I've distilled my experiences down to the few simple things that epitomize who I am, what I believe, and what's most important to me.

Results Through Personal Leadership

Leadership of people. Leadership of the business. Leadership of ideas. All three are on your shoulders. In interviews I always ask: "What simply would not have happened without you there?" (By the way, leadership of people helps net the other two leadership responsibilities.) Doing right by people is a deeply held value of mine.

Unbridled Passion and Collaboration

Passion. I tip great waitresses ludicrously well. Love what you do (whatever it is) and give it everything you've got. Express your creativity with vigor and create vigorous life experiences. Life's too short.

Collaboration. Everyone has something to offer. I don't know everything (not even close). But I know enough to know the power of listening and acting on others' ideas. It is a force multiplier beyond comparison. It's what caring humans do.

Fulfillment and Inspiration

My purpose and legacy in my professional life is to provide an environment that offers both. I love selling more widgets than last year, and it feeds my family. Creating fulfillment and inspiration feeds my soul.

Family and Fun

Family. My wife and daughter are amazing. Work is fantastic and I love it, but it doesn't define me. I define it.

Fun. I can't operate without humor; it's in my DNA.

Attitude and Integrity

Attitude. "Life is 10 percent what happens to you and 90 percent how you react to it," said inspirational author Charles Swindoll. Truer words were never spoken.[12]

Integrity. "In this lifetime, the only person you have to answer to is yourself"—from the movie *Rudy.*

Whether you call your declaration your Open Book Beliefs, your credo, or your guiding principles doesn't matter. What matters is that you have the thoughtfulness to *share it* early in your tenure. Indeed, any time you start a new managerial role you should take the opportunity to demonstrate thoughtfulness and connectedness on many fronts.

Foremost, you need a plan to land with authority, take the reins, and get off to a fast start. I will leave the idea of a classic "first 100 days" plan to other books written on this topic. Rather, I will focus on how your opening salvo as a manager new to an organization can promote meaning-making, fulfillment, and ultimately, higher performance. In such an instance, consider being very intentional about how you embed your new organization into your own first 100 days approach. It is critical to incorporate an others-focused mindset into the more standard "What do I need to create/establish/command/control?" mindset if you want to maximize trust and felt confidence in you and further help accelerate the formation of meaningful bonds.

I've developed a blueprint to help new managers craft an organizationally friendly beginning to their tenure; it's something I refer to in seminars as The BOSS: Blueprint for an Organizationally Savvy Startup.

It details seven ways—one for each of the Markers of Meaning—for you to quickly put the organization at the forefront and jump-start your meaning-making efforts.

THE BOSS
(Blueprint for an Organizationally Savvy Startup)
✳ ✳ ✳

1. *Provide an affirming outsider perspective and early prioritization (helps trigger the first Marker of Meaning—doing work that matters).* As a manager new to an organization, you bring a new perspective to the table. As part of this fresh lens on things, you can reinforce how the work an organization is doing really matters for the company, and why it matters. A new articulation of this belief can reconnect employees with the felt importance of their work. In addition, you can signal that you want to understand what work has the biggest impact and thus should be prioritized. This approach diffuses concerns that you will be the person who tries to do everything and instead assures the team that you place importance on doing work that matters most. Treating individual employee work plans as critical right up front also sends the right signal.

2. *Share stories of observed organizational learning and growth (helps trigger the second Marker of Meaning—being congruently challenged).* Early in your tenure, you can indicate just how important learning and growth is to you. You can relate your observations about where the organization has clearly learned something important and grown from it—even if it meant some pain along the way. Sharing such stories with a sense of appreciation and passion indicates to the new organization that learning and growth are priorities for you—which is good news for employees looking for more meaning in their workweek.

3. *Tell stories of admiration upon entry (helps trigger the third Marker of Meaning—working with a heightened sense of competency/self-esteem).* An easy early step for you to build meaning is to express admiration for the work, workers, or working environment associated with your new home. Hearing from an outsider what is impressive about a work group, and why it's impressive, helps to reinforce feelings of self-confidence and competence. It also sets a tone of respect coming from you. Even if you are taking over a troubled operation, there are certainly going to be areas of strength that can be praised and built on.

4. *Conduct multilevel onboarding interviews (helps trigger the fourth Marker of Meaning—being in control and influencing decisions/outcomes).* Change is hard enough on an organization; change without any sense of control is even worse. If you take the time early in your tenure to solicit observations and input from all levels of your new organization, and are personable about it, talking to people one-on-one, you engender a truly win-win situation. The benefits to you are numerous—such interviews can unveil important themes, especially when a standard set of questions is used (e.g., What's working around here? What's not working?). An understanding of the culture of the work group emerges, as does an appreciation for each of the members met.

And the interviewees may well be astonished that you took the time to sit with them and solicit their point of view. They will feel heard and in touch with their new leader, and they will feel they are contributing to any forthcoming changes or quick decisions that are necessary for you to make. Early individual and meaningful connections thus get made.

5. *Make a cultural first impression of consequence (helps trigger the fifth Marker of Meaning—working in a caring, authentic, team-*

work-based culture). No sense in waiting to contribute to a meaning-making culture built on caring, authenticity, and teamwork. After all, a whole lot of sizing up will be going on as you and your new constituents intermingle—on both sides of the coin. You should seek early opportunities to give rewards and recognition, have authentic first interchanges, and affirm the importance of teamwork.

6. *Score quick wins, and share a directional agenda (helps trigger the sixth Marker of Meaning—feeling a connection with and confidence in leadership and the mission).* Employees want to feel confidence in and a connection with their new leader, and fast. It's one of the most surefire ways to reassure employees that their work matters and is supporting something worthwhile, and to bolster a sense of belongingness and interconnectivity. Applying the insight in this chapter is a great place to start. You should also keep in mind the importance of establishing early wins and putting in place a directional agenda as soon as possible. As Michael Watkins, author of *The First 90 Days*, indicates, early wins "create a pervasive sense that good things are happening."[13] It is this pervasive sense that leads employees to have an early sense of confidence in you.

Similarly, employees don't want to wait for you to emerge from a 100-day sequestering armed with all the answers. Instead, you can share a directional agenda about early key areas of focus to serve as a placeholder while you are developing a more comprehensive growth plan. Such efforts dispel unproductive guesswork as to your agenda and help create confidence and connectedness sooner rather than later.

7. *Symbolically stop a worst-offender behavior (helps trigger the seventh Marker of Meaning—being free from corrosive workplace behaviors).* By connecting with multiple levels of the organization, one-on-one, as early and broadly as possible, you will have a good handle on the culture already in place. This process may well lead to identification of obvious corrosive behaviors that must stop. Visibly heading off at least one such behavior right out of the gate can be an early indication that you will tolerate positives only, not negatives, to the culture. (The concept of corrosive behaviors will be covered in depth in Chapter 9.)

Another crucial moment when you can deliver an incredibly motivating or demotivating message occurs during times of adversity. These times reveal our true character. Use them as an opportunity to show the strength of yours. Too often managers don't. They forget how many people take cues from them. They get caught in the storm instead of being the calm eye of the storm. A plant suffers a big quality incident and energy turns to finger pointing versus future prevention. A manager lashes out publicly at a team for having missed a critical deadline. Another manager distances herself from a vital failed initiative instead of owning her part in it and helping the team move forward. Still another manager adds to unproductive gossip in the face of rumored layoffs or budget cuts instead of being a calming influence.

Not wanting to fall prey to any situations of adversity such as these, early in my career I developed what I think of as my adversity manifesto. Any time I start a new role it's one of the first things I share with my organization, along with my Open Book Beliefs.

This *In Times of Adversity* manifesto announces to the organization several things:

There will most certainly be adversity in my tenure—it is life in the business world.

There are certain behaviors you can expect out of me in those tough times. Hold me to them.

I expect the same behaviors from you.

IN TIMES OF ADVERSITY

✳ ✳ ✳

✳ Be the eye of the storm. A calm, cool, and collected leader is a beacon. Never forget how many others take cues from you.

✳ Realize adversity reveals true character. Leverage it as a chance to show yours. It's one of the most lasting impressions you'll ever leave.

✳ Drive out fear. Job number one is to steer the ship back on course. There will be time later to constructively learn from who did/didn't do what. And remember, we really are all in this together. Our mortal enemy is ignorance of the fact that the enemy is external.

✳ Assemble a small, nimble coalition of experts for broad problem solving but quick action. Roll up your sleeves and flow to the work. Overcommunicate.

✳ Pull on that chain of command to help. Chains exist to provide added strength in times of need. That's why it's not called a "thread of command."

✳ Always remember, this too shall pass. It always does. It just passes faster when you use these principles.

Write your own version of an adversity manifesto. Reinforce to the troops that they can count on you to be a beacon even in the worst of storms. Make meaning for them when it's needed most.

The final specialty messaging situation applies to leadership teams. Leadership teams can often serve as the lynchpin for cultural reinforcement (or destruction). People who pass through leadership teams as part of project milestones, reviews, or checkpoints all have experiences that can build their confidence, self-esteem, and felt competence, or not. People can leave leadership team meetings feeling better connected and supported, or disconnected and unsupported. If you sit on such a leadership team, you can put some governance in place to ensure that the organization's experiences with the leadership team are supportive and culture enhancing by design, as opposed to haphazard and undermining.

The truth is that leadership teams forge meaningful connections with their constituents by being aware of and intentional about the quality of interactions they have with those constituents—not unlike how brands carefully plan the impressions they make on consumers. These brand impressions can continually reinforce the brand's equity or erode it. Do all Volvo communications reinforce the brand's core equity of safety? Do all of Coca-Cola's communications reinforce the core equities of refreshment and happiness?

Similarly, leadership teams can define what they want to stand for in the eyes of their organization (the leadership team's equity), then work to continually and consistently reinforce that equity. As a member of such a team, you can help define points of difference the team wants to stand for to distinguish itself from an ordinary leadership team (again much like brands decide on points of difference to drive what will differentiate them from other brands). You can then encourage team members to be mindful of how they appear to others and intentional about the experiences that they want others in the organization to have each and every time they interact with the leadership team.

For inspiration, here's an example of how members of a leadership team might define their desired equity, their desired points of difference, and what they want the experience of each interaction between the team and any given organization member to be. Creating such definitions reminds leadership teams to focus on what the organization needs from them, not vice versa. You can lead the charge in creating such definitions.

✳ *Leadership Team Desired Equity.* We help make every project better and leave every employee feeling supported.

* *Leadership Team Desired Points of Difference.* We fuel big results, big ideas, big discipline, big legacies, and big fun.

* *Leadership Team Visitors:*

  Observe—transparency, camaraderie, engagement

  Experience—support, respect/appreciation, infectious energy

  Leave with—clear direction/guidance, prioritization/tough calls made, barriers broken down

To keep these definitions truly active and alive, a leadership team (with your help) can create what I call an "authentic agenda" for its meetings, a modified version of the standard meeting agenda. Such an agenda has the leadership team's definitions of desired equity, points of difference, and experiences written right at the top of the agenda for a quick revisit at the beginning of each meeting, before the meeting topics of the day even start. The agendas can be made visible to all, and the organization is thus called on to help ensure the leadership team is authentically living up to its promises on paper.

* * *

As a leader, your role in enabling and framing meaning is irrefutable. Through your conduct and communications, you help others find meaning in and at work. Armed with knowledge of the meaning-making leadership traits and equipped with messaging savvy, you are even better equipped now to lead the way.

CHAPTER 9

Cutting Off
Corrosive Behaviors

SO FAR THIS BOOK HAS FOCUSED ON THE POSITIVE WAYS YOU CAN create meaning at work. These methods will all be for naught, though, if you don't address the negative behaviors that can drain employees of meaning. Social psychologists Steven Heine, Tracy Proulx, and Kathleen Vohs have found that when we are robbed of meaning or face meaningless conditions, we try to reconstruct meaning—often in other pockets of our work life or life in general.[1] But when we're striving to compensate, we aren't striving to elevate, thereby disrupting an organization and dragging down performance.

Where to start looking first?

The mirror.

You might not realize, given all your good intentions, that you could also be engaging in negative, meaning-draining behaviors. But if you are, you can be sure your employees realize it.

Research shows that managers can unwittingly kill meaning in four primary ways. I call them the Components of Corrosion.

1. Destroying a sense of certainty

2. Destroying a sense of completion

3. Destroying a sense of confidence

4. Destroying a sense of community

When any of these components are enacted, it creates self-doubt, deflates a sense of devotion, and causes us to question the meaning in and at work: We start wondering, "What's going on here?" "What's the point?" "Do I belong here?"[2] It can also contribute to fear: fear born of mistreatment, insecurities, ambiguity, or lack of understanding.

When you are aware of and intentionally cut off such behaviors you effectively trigger the seventh Marker of Meaning—freeing an organization from corrosive workplace behaviors and removing barriers to the best self.

DESTROYING A SENSE OF CERTAINTY

In their research, Heine, Proulx, and Vohs describe us as meaning makers, driven to make connections, find patterns, and establish associations in places where they may not inherently exist. We are compelled to bind ourselves to the external world and have a fundamental motivation to believe that our perceptions, attitudes, and behaviors are correct. When elements of our perceived reality are shattered, a disconcerting sense of fundamental incongruity motivates us to reestablish a sense of normalcy, coherence, and certainty.[3] This feeling of incongruity can be deeply unsettling; for example, when men set off explosives at a marathon race or police open fire on peaceful protesters. That is not how our world is supposed to be. We seek to make sense of the situation and reconfirm meaning elsewhere in our lives when such tragedies occur. We need to be certain of something, anything, in moments following such heinous events.

Albeit to a lesser degree, obviously, the same phenomenon happens when we destroy an employee's sense of certainty by not only creating fear but by acting without integrity, being indecisive or inconsistent, mismanaging change, or communicating poorly. Managers are not supposed to do these things, so when employees sense incongruity with the way things are supposed to be, it causes frustration, discomfort, disengagement, and a hasty search to reconnect with other, more meaningful frameworks in their lives. Let us now look at each of these corrosive behaviors and the corresponding antidotes.

Lack of Integrity

Integrity is as close to a nonnegotiable as there is in the business world and in life. Because it is expected (simply "the way it is supposed to be"), in theory it should be difficult to stand out for acting with integrity in business. Ironically, though, we've all seen enough violations of integrity that the smallest, everyday act of integrity can stand out and restore faith in the system.

Similarly, the smallest breach of integrity will stand out, each and every time, for the wrong reasons—in ways that absolutely destroy faith. The Lehman Brothers and Bernie Madoffs of the world get the most notoriety for how broadly their lack of integrity affects people. In our personal lives, however, even a small breach makes us uncertain about an individual or an organization, and that uncertainty is incredibly difficult to dissipate.

The great majority of us probably think that we have unimpeachable integrity. It's others who lack it. Integrity expert Dan Coughlin points out, however, that we all can improve ourselves by acting with internal integrity (i.e., being vigilant to always do what's right, even when no one is looking); acting with external integrity (i.e., doing what you say you will); integrating your internal and external integrity, so you don't come across as "fake" or inconsistent; and being mindful of your image of integrity (i.e., don't do things that are perfectly innocent but might cause someone watching to "wonder what's going on").[4] A little vigilance on these fronts can help protect an employee's sense of certainty and prevent faith, trust, and meaning from being obliterated.

Indecision

When a decision is not made, of course that is a decision. I once had a colleague who would good-naturedly ask anyone who was wavering, "Is your indecision final?" The idea, of course, is to approach each decision with a sense of finality.

So why don't we? What causes our indecision?

A desire for more data is pragmatic, but when overdone, it can quickly cross over to perfectionism. This desire to make the perfectly informed decision can grind decision making to a halt. As can the failure of the deciding body to feel a sense of accountability. Fear of making a wrong decision comes into play as well—fear that someone will be unhappy with the outcome or fear of the repercussions of a wrong decision. We can also lose sight of what the objective or goal behind the decision is in the first place, confusing ourselves in the process and likely overcomplicating the choice to be made.

If we don't take the time to thoroughly understand the options presented, we may delay making a decision that could have been made earlier if only we'd done our due diligence. Some of us lack the confidence to make a firm decision. Still others want it all and are unwilling to compromise until they see an option that contains no trade-offs.

Whatever the cause of the uncertainty, one thing is certain—the corrosive effect is inescapable.

Indecision can paralyze an organization. It can create doubt, uncertainty, lack of focus, and even resentment. Multiple options can linger, sapping an organization's energy and killing a sense of completion as well. Timelines stretch while costs skyrocket. Those costs can include a quicker, more aggressive competitor eating your lunch while the indecisive manager considers whether to use his fork or spoon.

Ron Thomas, a chief human resources officer and an advisory council member at *Harvard Business Review*, likens indecision to the plight of the wildebeest. "The wildebeest waits at the edge of the water trying to decide when to cross the river; however, each time there are some in the herd that will make a decision and be the first few to attempt the crossing. They are the ones that consistently get to the other side," he writes. "The indecisive ones that wait until the masses jump in suffer a higher fatality rate by the crocodile."[5]

So how do you avoid the brutally negative effects of indecision?

Well, of course the most obvious action is to just take a stand. Literally.

A study led by a team of clinical psychologists found a connection between our actual body movements and the state of our certainty when making a decision. Study participants read two separate articles about getting rid of a minimum wage for adults. One article simply stated the case for abolishing it; the other listed specific pros and cons for both sides of the argument. While reading the article, participants were asked to stand on a Wii Balance Board, a step platform used to enable interactive gaming through movement. One can snowboard on-screen, for example, by standing on the board and emulating the movements required for actual snowboarding. The Wii Balance Board was used in this case to measure the movement from side to side as each participant read one of the articles.

The study found that those reading the article with pros and cons were actually (though subconsciously) leaning from one side to the other more than those reading the more "fixed position" article. In times of indecision, where we are mentally vacillating, our bodies really do reflect that internal conflict via subtle side-to-side movement. The study participants were eventually asked to "take a stand" and state if they were for or against abolishing a minimum wage for adults, and the results showed that they tended to actually stand firm when stating their decision.

Interestingly enough, the reverse held true as well. In phase two of the study, participants were told they were engaged in a study of tai-chi movements. Those who were told to conduct more side-to-side movements showed more indecisiveness than those who were told to move up or down or make no movements at all.

So we move from side to side when we are uncertain, and the action of moving from side to side makes us feel more uncertain.[6]

So to free yourself from indecision, take a stand—literally.

Now, of course, if only it were that easy. Holding still when deciding will subconsciously strengthen your state of certainty, to be certain, but there's obviously more at play here. I share the story of this study (and the bit of misdirect) to indicate just how deeply engrained and hardwired our struggle to make a decision can run—and why the difficulty reverberates all the way down to subconscious body movements!

To truly overcome indecision requires thoughtful tactics of discipline that address more deep-seated causes. What follows are eight such tactics to help you both dig deep and get practical, moving from indecision to precision.

1. *Meter your emotions.* Sometimes our emotions can get in the way of making a decision, causing us to gloss over facts right in front of us or creating a desperate search for information to support the decision we really want to make. Countering indecision may require accepting inevitabilities much sooner while refusing to let emotions cloud the realities at hand. The fact is, being aware of your emotions and not letting them hijack the decision-making process is an important counterresponse to the stasis of indecision. By the way, there is nothing wrong with letting your heart (or gut) be the tiebreaker in making your decision; it's just critical that the head, heart, and gut all serve the process in a balanced, efficient fashion.

2. *Step back and evaluate the true impact of a wrong decision.* Fear of making an incorrect decision can paralyze us. At such times, it is helpful to step back and ask, "What is the worst thing that could happen in the long run if this decision turns out to be wrong?" Taking time to consider this broader perspective will often unveil that the consequences aren't that dire after all, and may well net much more decisiveness. Getting comfortable with the possibility of being wrong can actually help the right decisions happen faster. And remember these words of advice from a former colleague of mine: "You make decisions—decisions don't make you." That is, as long as you also keep in mind what another colleague reminded me of: "You just have to be right 51 percent of the time."

3. *Consider the risks/costs of not doing something.* Asking the question, "What are the risks/costs of not making a decision?" may create awareness of the pitfalls that would otherwise be glossed over. It may become obvious that budgets will run over, that competitors will gain precious time for counterplans, or that resources will have to be further stretched and kept from working on some other priority. Having this awareness will make you think twice before deciding not to decide.

4. *Act with self-assurance.* Self-doubt or worrying about what others expect you to decide can cripple a decision in progress. Self-confidence helps bolster the internal fortitude to make the tough calls, as well as the external reception of the decision once made. Ever watch someone visibly riddled with self-doubt arrive at a decision? Most of the time these are the decisions that won't stick.

5. *Rediscover the plot.* Sometimes just stepping back and getting some distance from a problem and refreshing yourself on the importance or objective of a decision to be made can be tremendously helpful. What seemed like a huge call to be made might reorient itself and shrink vastly in size. Revisiting the objective behind the decision to be made may provide a useful reorientation and illuminate a very clear choice among a set of options. And granting some time, space, and distance can help the fog of being too close to clear, making way for a reenergized and decisive point of view to emerge.

6. *Don't vacillate in a vacuum; step back and seek advice.* Indecision can arise from the constant rehashing of the same set of data, input, or experiences. Therefore, indecision can be conquered with exposure to a new perspective from other stakeholders or from someone not as close to the decision. Having someone else to play devil's advocate, counter your biases, and bring different experiences to the table can help break the stalemate.

7. *Set time-bound parameters for making the call.* When left to our own devices, it is only natural for us to take as much time as we can to decide something. Establishing tension in the form of time limitations can help stimulate decision making. Concrete, time-bound parameters (with some teeth to them) can force the perfectionist or those who want it all to let go a bit, thus enabling a decision and avoiding the pen-alties of wandering past the deadline.

8. *Understand that sharp discussions net sharp decisions.* We've all been in meetings where a decision is supposed to be made, but in fact you are left with no sense of tangible forward progress. The discussion seems circular, someone hijacks the meeting and launches into an unfocused or politically motivated soliloquy, or everyone and anyone jumps in with points that aren't even fully on topic. These free-for-alls distract the decider and throw the decision-making process off course. As a deciding manager, you need to be prepared to run a disciplined and pointed meeting that drives toward a decision by asking the right ques-tions, controlling the discussion flow, reining others in when necessary, and expanding discussion where appropriate to get all the information, options, and points of view out on the table.

Encouraging honesty in the discussion is especially important to avoid another kind of indecision—decisions that don't stick. We've all been a part of polite decision meetings where everyone is silent or silently head nodding, but they aren't actually in agreement and later indicate as much through their words and actions. This behavior is toxic in its own way because it yields decisions by default rather than by debate. A voice unheard can mean a decision undone.

Inconsistency

By definition, inconsistent leaders strip certainty from an organiza-tion. Dr. David De Cremer from Maastricht University in the Nether-lands confirmed in his studies that inconsistent leaders do indeed generate feelings of uncertainty in their subordinates, as well as appre-hension about future interactions with their offending manager. De Cremer's studies also showed that inconsistent leaders can actually damage their subordinates' self-esteem and are viewed as patently unfair, which can cause further self-doubt about future interactions.[7] Inconsistent behavior from leaders confuses people, erodes trust, causes fear, and can lead to a sort of learned inertia where the employee, paralyzed by uncertainty, just avoids or shuts down interactions with the offending manager.

So how does it happen? How does inconsistency come into play? Surely we don't set out with the goal of keeping our employees guessing.

The hard truth is that we are often unaware that our behaviors are being perceived as inconsistent. It does not help that as managers we live in a fishbowl, where our every action is seen by all. Furthermore, we may not realize how damaging our unintentional inconsistencies may be. To help, here are a half-dozen ways to overcome any tendency of inconsistency.

1. *Put your priorities on a pedestal.* Nothing will create more uncertainty and confusion for an organization than inconsistent messaging on strategies, vision, and goals (organizational priorities). The same holds true when you act inconsistently relative to your personal priorities at work, such as your stated beliefs, personal purpose, or desired legacy. Putting these priorities on a pedestal and constantly filtering decisions and actions relative to these priorities is what I call demonstrating critical consistency. It may require a personal campaign to strengthen your resolve. It might require an effort to stop trying to please everyone and be mindful to not always let the last word in your ear, well, last.

2. *Imagine a camera in the corner.* This is a simple exercise to help you spot your own inconsistencies. Imagine there is a camera in the corner of the room every time you are giving direction, making a decision, or interacting with someone in a certain situation. Reviewing the film later should not unveil a host of continuity problems; the world should see you acting in a manner consistent with your beliefs, actions, strategies, and goals.

3. *Think "see-say."* In advertising parlance, when developing a commercial it is critical that what the words are trying to communicate in each frame match what the picture is communicating (i.e., the "see" and the "say" match)—otherwise confusion sets in; after all, you only have thirty seconds to get your message across. It's the same for us as managers: Our visible actions should always match up with our words or else people will become confused and begin to tune out. Relatedly, a brand that doesn't follow through on its promises will never be bought again. And managers who don't follow through on what they say they will do will never have anyone buy into them (their decisions and direction) again, either.

4. *Mind your mood swings and impulses.* Inconsistent moods yield tentative employees and can even cause fear if the mood swings to downright nasty. Everyone, of course, is allowed different temperatures on different days. It's about being aware and minimizing the height and depth of the peaks and valleys, and perhaps even acknowledging when you are not your usual self. When someone's foul moods keep popping up periodically, other people may avoid or overly agree with the person, conceding and nodding in an effort to not trigger an explosion. Similarly, acting on impulse, either positively or negatively, can create touchy situations. Suddenly laying praise on someone loudly and openly when that's not your usual MO can cause suspicion. That's not to discourage acts of positivity, but you may have to telegraph why you are doing it now and reconcile why it's different from how you usually approach such situations. On the other side of the coin, impulsive outbursts of negativity can create fear and self-doubt.

5. *Know that same situation, different treatment doesn't work.* People will remember if similar situations produced different results and if managers interpret rules and policies differently to meet their own desired end; these inconsistencies may even raise doubts of integrity. This call for disciplined behavior shouldn't be viewed as at odds with the need for open-mindedness, the need to react to new data, or the need to flex your leadership behavior according to different situations. Rather, it is about the need for you to heighten your situation awareness and to be cognizant of the consistency of your behaviors and actions. The same goes for treatment of people; employees want to be treated fairly, not fairly inconsistently. Favoritism will fester into resentment, as will punishment that's not equally administered.

6. *Put repeatable processes in place.* You shouldn't let your crazy calendar and overpacked days dictate how you make decisions. Nor should you let such factors breed an environment where inconsistency is a natural by-product of harried actions. Chapter 6 provides inspiration for implementing a disciplined decision-making and activity process that will enable greater managerial consistency (and greater enrichment for those involved). Likewise, the adversity manifesto concept from Chapter 8 will help ensure consistent and predictable behavior even in times of crisis—a slice of time in which it is all too easy to stray from desired behavioral patterns.

Mismanagement of Change

When change is happening to us, our natural instinct is to work feverishly to reconstruct our new reality and to recover our sense of certainty about the world we are operating in. Studies show it is important for us as humans to make sense of the way things are about to be. Psychological doubt about what the change will mean leads to higher turnover and lower job satisfaction. Most important, organizational psychologists have discovered that if employees can't make a link between change and their own personal goals and values (or, worse, if a direct conflict exists between them), the intrinsic motivation and associated meaning derived from work disappears.[8] Similarly, change can challenge the identities employees have built, also draining meaning in the process. For example, plant technicians who have proudly built mastery with one machine type may find their identities as experts challenged with the influx of the next generation of machinery.

Employees must be able to make sense of and assign personal meaning to the changes taking place, or their sense of certainty is compromised and they will resist the changes in the short term and spiral downward in the longer term.

And the fundamental problem behind change doesn't make things any easier. Companies are worried about sustaining the business during change, while employees are understandably worried about keeping their jobs. Interests are aligned but they aren't mutual. This adds to the likelihood that change will be executed in a fashion that simply doesn't work for the employee.

While much has been written on change management, I want to focus on how to maintain meaning during the process of change management. Being cognizant of meaning-maintenance during change is the surest way to not only bring about acceptance of the change, but to ensure the change integrates into an overall plan for sustained performance over time. In this sense, the mismanagement of change can be avoided. Here are five ways, then, to maintain meaning during the process of change management.

1. *Defuse fear of the unknown.* An up-front commitment to be up front in communicating change is essential. Providing the information needed at the onset of change and even overcommunicating, while being honest about what isn't known yet, can keep change from negatively altering the meaning derived at work. Our minds fill in the blanks when information is lacking; new realities that employees begin to construct in their minds might be built on the wrong foundation. In the absence of proper information and context, as employees try to make sense of the change, emotional and rational reactions can swing wildly out of control. Frequent updates throughout the process of change, even when everything isn't known, can go a long way to defusing fear. You shouldn't underestimate the maturity of employees to be able to handle work-in-progress communications; nor should you underestimate the immaturity that can take hold in the face of radio silence. All in all, committing to a disciplined communication plan behind change can eliminate fear of the unknown, fear of hidden agendas, and even fear of failure.

2. *Make a clear case for change.* Without such a case, it will look like what change management expert Jim Clemmer calls "management by whim."[9] An abundance of clear, sound logic can help employees to make sense of the change. Helping them understand the risk of staying stagnant versus changing can also help on this front. With a clear-cut case for change that's well communicated, employees can quickly buy in and move on to reconstructing their new reality in a way that preserves and enhances the meaning they derive from work.

3. *Frame the change.* Helping employees to see how change links to their personal goals and values and how it can strengthen the identities they are building is one of the most powerful ways to maintain meaning during the change management process. Employees need to understand not only how change affects them, but how change can affect an even better version of them. Clearly linking the change to learning and growth opportunities can magnify meaning during the process. This is also true of helping employees understand how rewards will match or exceed the efforts that will be required as a result of the change. Employees themselves also obviously play a big part in maintaining or bolstering meaning during the implementation of change. They may need to get out of their comfort zone, adapt their identity a bit, or adjust their goals a little.

4. *Involve them in the construction of change.* I've heard it said and found it true that a change imposed is a change opposed. Change that happens to people, rather than change they are a part of, is perceived as a loss of control. Making an effort to involve people affected by change early and often (as much and as widely as is practical) maintains their deep-seated need to have a sense of control. It also provides more time for those who will be affected by the change to process what it will mean and how they might forge positive links to their personal goals, values, and identities. Those involved in the construction of change can also help create effective mechanisms to carry out the change in an acceptable, nonchaotic fashion.

5. *Equip them for change.* When people don't feel they are ready for change, it can challenge their felt certainty and competency, which in turns affects self-confidence and strips the intrinsic motivation of work. Feeling ill-equipped for change is inconsistent with the meaning-making goals and values of learning and growing. Resources and training required should be mapped out carefully before change is even announced. And change agents can be recruited to help role-model the new skills and behaviors required, thus providing much-needed reassurance.

Lack of Communication/Listening

George Bernard Shaw once said, "The single biggest problem in communication is the illusion that it has taken place."[10] Therein lies the problem: In environments where communication is poor, we are either not investing the time it takes to communicate effectively, we believe communication is happening at a sufficient level when in fact it is not, or we are simply not listening well. Communication all too often breaks down not only because the sender isn't really sending but because the receiver isn't really receiving. A sense of certainty will ultimately and undoubtedly be compromised in such an environment.

Accordingly, the potential for a trickle-down negative impact on meaning, fulfillment, and performance is too great to not get all this right.

The solution is to take the time to invest in communication, care enough to inquire, and then listen. Mary Kay Ash built an entire cosmetics empire around a simple philosophy: "Everyone has an invisible sign around their neck that says, 'Make me feel important.'"[11]

One of the most powerful ways to make people certain that they are important to you is to inquire and listen. Regularly check in and ask how they are doing and see what is going on in their lives. Use a technique that I call P:60—which stands for "personal sixty seconds." Before the start of a regularly scheduled team meeting, go around the table asking each member to give sixty seconds of personal information, sharing something that's going on in their lives outside of work that will help others to see more of the whole person.

Similarly, ask Mike Michael about the power of listening—really listening—to facilitate high-quality communication and a corresponding high-quality result. Mike is president and CEO of Fifth Third Bank's largest region. The bank went through a massive system conversion in 2013, condensing twenty-four types of checking accounts down into five. How could the bank keep the lines of communication open and ensure the net result maximally benefited the customer? Michael harnessed his reputation for being a genuine, caring listener and leader and took it to a whole new level.

He and his retail team launched a listening exercise conducted on a scale never before seen in the industry.

They talked and listened to over *300,000 people*, face-to-face.

They delved into life status and life objectives so that they could figure out the best ways to help. The result was an organization that's much more practiced in the art of carefully receiving communications, that is unequivocally certain about its client's needs, and that now has a much happier client base.

When you commit to the practice of listening, you too can create a much happier client base—your employees.

DESTROYING A SENSE OF COMPLETION

Ever notice how deeply unsatisfying it is when you are unable to complete a task you wanted to complete? As human beings we are driven in part by a sense of progress, a desire to see that our unique efforts are adding up to something tangible. We like to check the box and move on.

We can unwittingly stand in the way of this fundamental human drive with behaviors that destroy an employee's sense of ownership, behaviors that create rework, or behaviors that create wasted effort. Employees robbed of a sense of ownership are made to feel insignificant and untrusted. Employees experiencing rework or wasted effort develop a sense that unnecessary work and inefficient processes are getting in the way of completing other, more meaningful tasks. All of these actions rob employees of a feeling of accomplishment and a sense that their efforts have mattered—causing a sense of meaning to evaporate.

Killing Feelings of Ownership

Teresa Amabile and Steven Kramer of Harvard Business School have conducted studies that detail how managers at all levels routinely, and unwittingly, kill meaning at work with their words and actions. Their research indicates that managers can destroy a sense of ownership by switching people off projects before their work is completed or by shifting goals so frequently that people despair that their work will ever see the light of day.[12] Being aware of these triggers can help you to avoid them.

You can also destroy a sense of ownership when you jump in too soon or do too much for an employee. When this occurs, the employee gets a sense that the work completed was in fact someone else's. It can be very tricky to discern where the line is; when is doing something to assist the employee too much? In general, if you ever say to yourself, "Oh, I'll just do it for them," resist doing just that. Employees have to be able to make and learn from mistakes, and still feel supported along the way. It is a balancing act, but getting that balance right starts with awareness of the need for employees to be given a chance.

Furthermore, you can destroy an employee's sense of ownership when you miss the opportunity to reaffirm the employee's leadership role in something in front of others. Holding court with business partners without first steering them to the employee, as well as failing to have the employee's back, hurts credibility and undermines the sense of ownership you want the employee to experience.

Finally, deploying an objective and then not managing by objective (and micromanaging instead) also crushes an employee's sense of ownership and should be avoided at all costs.

Creation of Rework and Waste

If what we do really matters, it makes meaning. The exact antithesis of this, then, is work that is literally wasted, has no point, or is done twice.

It's hard to imagine anything that matters less. And it isn't the workers who typically cause this violation of meaning—it's their managers.

No one sets out to create rework and waste, and yet it happens. Why?

One culprit is when we give unclear or imprecise direction up front. Another is when we fail to get our chain of management aligned to something, which then triggers substantive work later. Lack of respect for people's time causes us to be late or engage in behaviors that effectively waste time. A desire to exhaustively cover every angle leads to work that ultimately is done without a useful purpose. Indecision and insecurity plays its part as well, as does overreacting to new developments.

The bottom line is that this behavior kills the sense of completion that human beings are deeply drawn to. Repeating or reworking a task is inherently bereft of fulfillment because the human mind can't resist drawing the conclusion that the first go-around, or any go-around, didn't matter. Completed work that is a complete waste causes frustration and drains meaning. And I'm not referring to work that was ultimately discarded but served as a valuable learning experience and stepping stone along the way. I'm talking about lazy behavior causing unnecessary rework and waste—something that simply has no place in a meaning-making organization.

Asserting control over these specific corrosive behaviors requires awareness of three power questions we can ask ourselves:

1. *Did I give a clear brief for the work?* Businesses all the way from advertising agencies to military organizations require a clear brief for the mission before they get started. What is the objective of the work? What are the expectations? Who is doing what? Are all the stakeholders of the work's outcome aligned to the work to be done? An undisciplined approach to the assignment of work will lead to great inefficiency and wasted effort and energy.

2. *Is the juice worth the squeeze?* This question (introduced in Chapter 7) helps us to get serious about simplification, and it is certainly applicable here. Asking for work in an effort to cover every angle is not exhaustive thinking—it's exhaustively lazy thinking. And it hints at underlying insecurities, which cannot be the driving force behind requests for work. Each new piece of work requested should be carefully viewed through the filter of whether it's truly worth doing. The bottom line here is that you must realize you could be asking someone to do something that is literally meaningless. That is the exact opposite of bringing more meaning to the workplace.

Of course, you have to consider new information along the way that could trigger new or different work. However, this is about choosing not to do the easy thing by doing everything, but instead being disciplined enough to choose only the worthy things to work on. Such a mindset helps ensure no effort is wasted.

3. *Am I acting with an abundant scarcity mentality?* People have limited time, resources, and energy. Respect for those scarcities should be abundant. Wasteful behavior here causes missed opportunity for a sense of completion realized elsewhere.

DESTROYING A SENSE OF CONFIDENCE

Research indicates that dismissing the importance of an employee's ideas or work can crush a sense of self-confidence and accordingly a sense of meaning for the employee.[13] This can occur whether the work is overtly dismissed or even if there is simply a failure to recognize the importance of one's contributions.

The same is true of overly critical or punishing behavior such as unduly harsh feedback, overemotional reactions, a nothing-is-ever-good-enough mindset, or plain callousness—all of which can induce the question, What's the point? Criticized employees start to wonder if they are truly valued and respected or if they will ever match up to the overbearing boss's expectations. It's hard for our employees to find meaning and fulfillment at work when doubt continually creeps in for them and they start wondering whether they are even fulfilling our base expectations.

Let's further examine this particular set of corrosive behaviors and the corresponding offsets.

If you are quick to criticize and slow to praise, don't be surprised if your employee's work needs criticizing and isn't worth praise. I can recommend six ways to help keep you from exhibiting overcritical and callous behavior at work, thus avoiding the potential to compromise an employee's sense of self-confidence.

1. *Assume they care about doing good work.* Criticism about someone else's work is often born out of frustration and assumptions that the other person lacks regard for doing the job right. Don't assume that, and plain and simple, stop being so critical. There is simply no substitute for giving the benefit of the doubt and building corrective comments on a foundational belief that others want to do their best. People generally want to shine, not shirk.

2. *Don't create the need for neutralization.* When people get harshly criticized they tend to engage in a number of tactics to neutralize the sting. They will do things like seek out other people's opinions, withdraw and take recovery time, console themselves that their manager doesn't define them, or look for validation elsewhere. An ounce of prevention is required here. Imagine sending someone off forced to soothe the bite of brittle feedback, and anticipate that you could cause this scenario if you aren't careful. This will remind you to apply a filter to avoid unduly harsh feedback.

3. *Plant seeds of growth, not seeds of doubt.* Related to the above but worthy of separate consideration is the thought that criticism should be given and framed in a way to actually encourage nurturing and growth. The idea is to give constructive, not destructive, feedback and to avoid creating self-confidence setbacks.

4. *Don't manufacture misattribution; share context.* There is a good chance that criticism poorly delivered from you will be rejected by the recipient and attributed to any unkind perceptions the recipient might have about you, thereby widening an existing rift or unintentionally causing a new one. Context can often be missing—context that, if you shared and clarified, would improve receptivity of the well-intended criticism. Instead, package criticisms with thoughtful explanations of why the criticism is being offered and how it could help the individual. By depersonalizing the criticism you will turn it from overbearing to overflowing with good intent.

5. *Better self-manage anxiety/stress.* Criticism of others often comes from our insecurities or inability to manage our own anxieties and stress. Better managing these forces can make us better managers— ones that don't subconsciously project our own insecurities by defaulting to criticism of others (and thus causing insecurities to arise in others as well).

6. *Warm up.* Yup, this means stop being an ice queen or king. This can create doubts in your employees' minds about how you are perceiving them. People can read a lack of compassion and warmth a mile away, and they will stay a mile away when they sense it.

DESTROYING A SENSE OF COMMUNITY

As we established in Chapter 7, people seek to have close and lasting relationships with others at work and in general work in a caring environment. They want to feel they belong to a community. We strip our employees of this sense of community when we allow environments of negativity to persist and unhealthy levels of internal competition to exist. Sensing that they are in combat, not in a community, employees may well mentally shut down at work and seek paths elsewhere in order to find less resistance and much more social reward. Meaning, fulfillment, and associated performance are thus undermined. A closer look is warranted at each of these damaging behaviors as well as at their corresponding remedies.

Negativity

The causes of negativity in the workplace are too many to count, but you can count on any one of them impacting the sense of community present in an organization. The multiplier effect that even one negative personality can have on an organization should be seen as too much to bear. Here are five manners by which you can keep such negativity at bay.

1. *Drive awareness of the behavior's impact.* Negative individuals might not realize the full extent of the corrosive impact they are having. Furthermore, it is critical to make it clear that the negative behavior won't be tolerated. In fact, it is your responsibility—after all, you will get the behavior you tolerate.

2. *Switch the "isms."* Go from pessimism to optimism. It sounds simple. But continually having to counter pessimists with positivity can be positively draining. Sticking at it, however, wears down the naysayer and reinforces to them that their negative behaviors are unwelcome. The pessimists may eventually get caught up in the optimism and thus vastly increase their capacity to contribute in a productive manner.

3. *Challenge cynics.* Cynics get their power when no one challenges them—their acidic statements can seem smart in the absence of a countering force. Challenge their statements and invite them to be a part of the solution instead. If they can't suggest solutions, they lose their power.[14]

4. *Don't let falsehoods and ferocity fester.* Speak up. Stating nothing in the face of falsehoods, unduly negative commentary, or vicious pessimism is as bad as adding to it. Don't get sucked into the orbit of negativity.

5. *Build people's self-image and redirect their energy.* Negative individuals may have a lot of negative things going on behind the scenes. Demonstrate empathy and find places to build their self-esteem. Get to work on redirecting their energy.

Excessive Internal Competitiveness

As the saying goes, a little competition is healthy. Too much competitiveness, focused internally, is most certainly not, however. It can show up as a variety of subversive behaviors, such as a lack of teamwork, backstabbing, one-upmanship, or even sheer sabotage. Any one of these behaviors can almost singlehandedly destroy a sense of community. Such behaviors can be rooted in organizational inequities like the unfair and unbalanced allotment of resources, including rewards and recognition. Similarly, when goals across functions and business units aren't aligned, it can create unnecessary internal competition. Selfishly focused or insecure individuals can be the root cause of such behavior as well. Counter these antics in three ways:

1. *Create a fair playing field.* We all just want a fair deal and to be dealt with fairly. When the rules are stacked against us, a game is no fun; if we still have to play we may look for ways to beat the rule makers rather than win the game. Do you want your employees fighting you or the competition?

2. *Drive a one-team, one-dream mindset.* Different goals mean different behaviors. These differing behaviors can quickly run counter to one another when they don't serve the same goal in the end. The same goals, if they stretch people and are inspiring enough, will draw an organization together, not split its employees apart.

3. *Redirect the energy of the overly aggressive or insecure.* Those who fritter away precious energy on protective, aggressive, or cover-up behaviors should be redirected to expend their energy on more positive pursuits. Overly aggressive, selfishly behaving individuals can be made to understand that their end-goals can

be achieved in another way—in a manner that helps them lift while they climb. The insecure can be made secure through attentiveness to actions that boost their self-esteem.

* * *

The Components of Corrosion are daunting foes. Be aware of these most toxic workplace behaviors and the ways in which they destroy a sense of meaning. Armed then with this awareness and the solutions provided in this chapter, you can cut these behaviors off wherever they appear or even before they begin to show themselves—either in yourself (as tough as it may be to admit) or anyplace up, down, or across the organization.

part five

DILIGENCE

CHAPTER 10

A Plan to Make It Matter

THERE ARE A LOT OF EXECUTABLE IDEAS AND CONCEPTS IN THIS book to help you create meaning *in* and *at* work. The two tools presented here will allow you to take all those ideas and organize them into a comprehensive plan tailored for your own situation and passion points.

THE MEANING-MAKING MENU

This first tool lays out all of the book's ideas and concepts according to the Marker of Meaning they trigger and the desired emotional connection or feeling they generate. You can pick from the list (Table 10-1) as your interests dictate.

Table 10-1. *The meaning-making menu.*

MARKER OF MEANING	DESIRED EMOTIONAL CONNECTION OR FEELING	EXECUTABLE IDEAS/CONCEPTS
DIRECTION		
1. DOING WORK THAT MATTERS (significant work that makes a real impact on you/the business/others, is reflective of your values and beliefs, and worthy of your focus and energy)	Enabling this condition means employees feel a deep sense of significance, satisfaction, connection, and commitment to their work and the higher-order point of it all. They feel they are serving who they are and what matters most to them.	**The Path to Purpose**—Discover how to bring the Profound Why of work to life using a very specific set of steps that will connect one to a higher-order end. **Purpose Power-Ups**—Use these two supplemental power sources for further help in creating a sense of purpose in one's work. **The Five Footprints of Legacy & The Five-Step Footpath to Legacy-worthy Results**—Learn to bring the Profound What to life by understanding the manner in which we tend to leave a lasting impact behind, and then the specific steps one can take to maximize the fulfilling legacy left behind via meaningful results. Several tools within tools help you sharpen the imprint.
DISCOVERY		
2. BEING CONGRUENTLY CHALLENGED (in ways that personally energize and maximize individual learning and growth) **3. WORKING WITH A HEIGHTENED SENSE OF COMPETENCY AND SELF-ESTEEM** (feeling valued and valuable, worthy and worthwhile)	Triggering these Markers means energizing employees. They feel the investment being made in their betterment and the underpinning of support they're being given. They experience a surge in felt competence and self-esteem as they grow and flourish, feeling more valuable and worthy all the while.	**Adult Learning Principles**—Discover the most workplace-applicable principles of adult learning and apply liberally. **How to Foster a Sense of Discovery at Work**—Ignite learning and a sense of discovery by being conducive to learning and engaging in these specific actions and behaviors. **Roles That Promote a Learning and Growth Environment**—Learning is maximized when you adeptly and flexibly vary the enabling roles you play ("metamorphosing") in the development of others. This list describes the variety of roles you can take on to further facilitate learning and growth. **Job Reimagining**—Think of work as a malleable set of building blocks you can reconfigure to better imbue meaning into your job, and learn how to make it happen. **How to Design Learning Exchanges**—Learning organizations encourage energetic exchanges among members to advance knowledge and growth. Find out how to design learning exchanges for maximum effectiveness with this list of ideas.

MARKER OF MEANING	DESIRED EMOTIONAL CONNECTION OR FEELING	EXECUTABLE IDEAS/CONCEPTS
DISCOVERY		**How to Construct a Thoughtful Learning Plan**—Use these three questions to unveil the subject matter for learning that strikes the deepest chords of inner congruence and fulfillment for the employee. **The Learning Loop**—Leverage this visual reminder to help break the employee out of a mere "do-loop" and instead guide him or her into a "learning loop"—a lifelong cycle of learning at work. **Lean Forward to Learn**—Remember this charge to seek out new learning experiences that stretch you and your employees.
4. BEING IN CONTROL AND INFLUENCING DECISIONS/ OUTCOMES (sense of autonomy)	Activating this Marker gives employees a sense of control, independence, ownership, and importance. They feel capable and even stretched as they are given opportunity to influence end results. They experience an even greater desire to affect a positive outcome.	**The Employee-Centered Decision-Making Method**—Follow these seven steps to conduct decision making in a manner that turns the process into an energizing productivity and morale boost. Learn how to place your employees at the center of the process and give them an opportunity for meaningful influence. **How to Grant Autonomy in a Way That Maximizes Meaning**—It takes work to give away work. Empowerment executed poorly can backfire and drain, not drive, meaning. This list contains eight ways to help you grant autonomy in an intelligent, effective fashion that avoids all the potential pitfalls.
5. WORKING IN A CARING/AUTHENTIC/ TEAMWORK-BASED CULTURE (feeling appreciated and wanting to bring one's whole self to work; having a sense of belongingness and harmony with coworkers, leaders, and company) **DEVOTION**	Forging this cultural underpinning and triggering this Marker results in employees feeling like they work in a tight-knit community. Employees will develop deep emotional bonds with each other and with their company. They will feel appreciated, respected, and cared for. They will experience a great sense of interconnectedness with their fellow employees and feel a harmonious connection with their true selves as well.	**Think Family Unit, Not Military Unit**—Remember this charge to inspire your day-to-day interactions with others and to maximize meaning derived from your relationships in the process. **Mantras for Meaningful R&R**—Start your campaign for rewards and recognition done right with these five principles. **How to Deliver Respectcognition**—You can provide meaningful day-to-day recognition by holding sacred the act of being respectful in your interactions with others. This list lays out the "thou shalt" reminders. **A SPECIFIC Plan**—Pinpoint specific steps to take in working toward achieving work-life harmony with this guide.

(continues)

(continued)

MARKER OF MEANING	DESIRED EMOTIONAL CONNECTION OR FEELING	EXECUTABLE IDEAS/CONCEPTS

DEVOTION

| | | **Enable Swell-Being**—You can supercharge meaning by visibly showing concern for the personal well-being of others. Learn the helping behaviors for enabling well-being and how to deliver them to help amplify (or swell) their effect.

How to Foster Authenticity—Remember the charge to help others be where they belong and to be true to themselves, as well as the "code of conduct" for specifically how to show up as being authentic. Such behaviors contribute heavily to a meaning-making culture.

How Teamwork Fosters Fulfillment—Recall the four ways that teamwork leads to a more fulfilled workforce and let them inspire your plan. Follow the specific set of behavioral expectations for creating a sense of interdependence, which will in turn maximize the level of teamwork and meaning derived. |
| **6. FEELING CONNECTION WITH AND CONFIDENCE IN LEADERSHIP AND THE MISSION** (and where you fit within it and how you can make a difference toward that mission) | Triggering this Marker makes employees feel like they are on the winning team. They will feel connected to their leader and the mission, and experience great confidence in both. Employees will encounter a deep sense of trust and pride in their leader, leadership team, and the company itself, and draw tremendous comfort from knowing that the leaders have their backs. They will be able to better make sense of things and will feel inspired that they can make a difference toward achievement of the mission at hand. | **The Traits of Meaning-Making Leaders**—Keep in mind these four characteristics of a high-connectivity, meaning-making leader and get to practicing "how to be."

How to Ensure Your Messaging Fosters Meaning—Meaning-making leaders communicate the right things, in the right way, to make their audience feel what they want them to feel. Master such messaging with this little helper.

My Open Book Beliefs—When you enter a new managerial role, use this tool to make it simple for the organization to get to know you, which eases fear of the unknown and helps get relationships off to a great start.

How to Jump-Start Meaning-Making in Your New Role—New bosses create new angst as employees try to figure out how their work lives will be affected. There are seven ways to hit the ground running that will quickly amp up meaning versus creating doubt (as detailed in the BOSS tool). |

MARKER OF MEANING	DESIRED EMOTIONAL CONNECTION OR FEELING	EXECUTABLE IDEAS/CONCEPTS
		The Adversity Manifesto—Great leaders know that how they respond in times of adversity reveals true character. Take advantage of these times to show your true character with help from this tool.
		Example of a Leadership Team's Desired Equity/Points of Difference/Visitor Experiences—Be inspired to ensure that meaning-making mindfulness is guiding the nature of interactions between a leadership team and the broader organization.
7. BEING FREE FROM CORROSIVE WORKPLACE BEHAVIORS (removing barriers to the best self)	Freeing an organization from corrosive conditions is a Marker that engenders a felt sense of certainty, completion, confidence, and community. Employees safeguarded from highly destructive behaviors effectively have barriers to their best self removed. They are free from fear and focused on development, growth, and delivering meaningful results. Their sense of belongingness is strengthened and the idea of work as a fulfilling and enjoyable entity is protected.	**Learn how to counter the four Components of Corrosion** (destroying a sense of certainty, completion, confidence, and community) by attacking the underlying, causal corrosive behaviors head-on: • **Improve Your Integrity**—Learn the four ways to improve on something you may have thought was a given. • **How to Address Indecision**—Move from indecision to precision with this list of thoughtful tactics of discipline that address the deep-seated causes of indecisiveness. • **How to Overcome Inconsistency**—Use these half-dozen methods to keep from crossing over from effective to erratic. • **How to Maintain Meaning During Change Management**—Discover how to help others make sense of change and assign personal meaning to the change taking place. • **Reversing a Lack of Communication and Listening**—Remember the charge to invest in communication, care enough to inquire, and simply listen. • **Maintaining Their Sense of Ownership**—This checklist reminder helps you to preserve an employee's sense of ownership and completion. • **How to Eliminate Rework and Waste**—You can employ three power questions to ensure that work being done is work that matters.

DEVOTION

(continues)

(continued)

MARKER OF MEANING	DESIRED EMOTIONAL CONNECTION OR FEELING	EXECUTABLE IDEAS/CONCEPTS
DEVOTION		• **How to Avoid Overcriticality and Callousness**—Being overcritical and callous is like a blunt force strike to one's sense of confidence and community. Let this list of ideas demonstrate another way forward. • **Neutralizing Negativity**—The multiplier effect of even one negative personality cannot be tolerated. Use the five ways listed to overcome this energy-sapping force. • **How to Diffuse Overcompetitiveness**—Learn how to diffuse unhealthy workplace competitiveness and transform it back into healthy competition.

You don't have to implement every activity on this menu; that would be impractical and overwhelming. Just pick the elements that stir your passion the most, and then weave those elements into a tailored but executable plan.

A STRUCTURED ACTION PLAN FOR MEANING-MAKING

The second tool will help you to create a personal to-do list for yourself, organized by groups of meaning-making activities. There are five buckets of activity for you to consider in this approach to structuring your action plan:

1. Overarching Behaviors (to be mindful of)

2. Skill Sharpening (to undertake)

3. Deep One-on-One Connections (to facilitate)

4. Systems (to put in place)

5. Group/Team Connections (to enable)

The grid in Table 10-2 represents a sample plan, laying out some of the executable ideas and concepts from this book and placing them into one of each of the five activity buckets.

Table 10-2. *Structured action plan for meaning-making.*
(SAMPLE PLAN)

Activity Bucket	Specific Action	Sample of Supporting Executable Ideas/ Concepts
1. Overarching Behaviors	Be mindful of How to Be (have a passion for potential; emit a caring/connective undercurrent; possess framing finesse; create an atmosphere of relaxed intensity) Maintain a sense of certainty, completion, confidence, and community (while avoiding corrosive behaviors)	✓ The Traits of Meaning-Making Leaders ✓ How to Address Indecision ✓ How to Overcome Inconsistency ✓ Neutralizing Negativity ✓ Maintaining Their Sense of Ownership
2. Skill Sharpening	Unlock rich learning Show up as maximally caring Accentuate authenticity at every turn Enhance meaning derived from messaging	✓ Adult Learning Principles ✓ How to Design Learning Exchanges ✓ The Learning Loop ✓ Mantras for Meaningful R&R ✓ How to Deliver Respect-cognition ✓ Enable Swell-Being ✓ How to Foster Authenticity ✓ How to Ensure Your Messaging Fosters Meaning ✓ How to Jump-Start Meaning-Making in Your New Role ✓ The Adversity Manifesto

(continues)

(continued)

Activity Bucket	Specific Action	Sample of Supporting Executable Ideas/ Concepts
3. Deep One-on-One Connections	Facilitate introspective and powerfully motivating reframing to find the Why and the What that matters most in one's work	✓ The Path to Purpose ✓ The Five Footprints of Legacy ✓ The Five-Step Footpath to Legacy-worthy Results
4. Systems	Put systems in place to engrain employees in the decision-making process and to enable them to have meaningful influence	✓ The Employee-Centered Decision-Making Method ✓ How to Grant Autonomy in a Way That Maximizes Meaning
5. Group/Team Connections	Facilitate a felt sense of meaningful interconnected-ness among group/team members	✓ How Teamwork Fosters Fulfillment

Like mileage, everyone's plan will differ. Choose the activities from each of the five buckets (as detailed throughout this book) that you find most inspiring, weave them into a tailored plan, and proceed accordingly.

M2 REVIEWS

With diligence done and a plan in place to truly make work matter, we next take on a time-honored workplace tradition: the performance review. You can do more than just conduct mere performance reviews; instead, you can conduct reviews that will ensure you Make It Matter. I call these M2 reviews. They go beyond the usual discussion of job performance to provide the opportunity for you and your employees to review progress against the holistic plan for making their work truly matter to them. Potential points of discussion for the M2 review are:

❋   Has the past year been successful in terms of triggering Markers of Meaning for employees?

* How fulfilled are the employees and just how elevated is their performance?

* Are employees experiencing new levels of energy and renewed passion for their work?

* Have employees identified a purpose and desired legacy and begun intentionally contributing to each?

* Do employees feel appropriately challenged? Have they learned/grown a lot over the past year?

* Have they done well with their autonomy and opportunities to influence?

* Do they feel appropriately appreciated, rewarded, and valued?

* Are they experiencing a strong sense of community and belonging?

* Are they feeling confident in and connected with leadership, the mission, and their ability to contribute to the mission?

* Do employees feel free from corrosive behaviors at work?

In a Make It Matter, or M2, review, such questions are the centerpiece of a much more robust discussion than a standard review would allow. The point is that the classic performance review discussion should not be limited to just the usual metrics of performance, but should instead expand to a much broader, more personal, and more introspective talk about what is creating meaning and fulfillment for the employee and how that is translating into new heights of performance. A mere performance review can't touch an M2 review in terms of keeping you and your employee maximally connected. Conducting M2 reviews at regular intervals also helps keep the employee on the path to delivering best-level performance and enjoying the tremendous intrinsic value that comes along with the pursuit.

OUR GREATEST ROLE

The net result of everything this book contains is the creation of great meaning and the fulfillment and truly profound performance that go along with it. Our greatest role as managers is to help others reach that state.

The truth is that work can be so much more for us. All the knowledge and tools are now at your disposal. We can make work truly work for us, on so many levels, when it truly matters.

May achievement of this elevated and exuberant state, for yourself and others, now be a mere matter of time.

Notes

INTRODUCTION

1. Warren Bennis, *Building a Culture of Candor: A Crucial Key to Leadership*, The Conference Board Annual Report (2004).

CHAPTER 1: WHY MEANING MATTERS

1. N. Blacksmith and J. Harter, *Majority of American Workers Not Engaged in Their Jobs*, Gallup (Oct. 28, 2011).

2. B. Chang et al., Conference Board Job Satisfaction Survey (June 2014); BlessingWhite Employee Engagement Research Update (Jan. 2013); and Towers Watson Global Workforce Study (2012).

3. BlessingWhite Employee Engagement Research Update.

4. Blacksmith and Harter, *Majority of American Workers Not Engaged in Their Jobs*.

5. L. Branham and M. Hirschfeld, *Re-Engage* (New York: McGraw-Hill, 2010), p. 28.

6. W. A. Kahn, "Psychological Conditions of Personal Engagement and Disengagement at Work," *Academy of Management Journal* 33, no. 4 (1990), pp. 692–724.

7. Kahn, "Psychological Conditions."

8. Ibid.

9. Christopher Bartlett quoted in B. Morris, *The New Rules*, Fortune.com, (Aug. 2, 2006).

10. L. Holbeche and N. Springett, *In Search of Meaning at Work*, Roffey Park Institute (2004), p. 3.

11. R. D. Arvey, I. Harpaz, and H. Liao, "Work Centrality and Post-Award

Work Behavior of Lottery Winners," *The Journal of Psychology* 130, no. 1 (2004).

12. J. Holtaway, "The Meaningful Workplace," *Emotive Brand.com* (May 30, 2012).

13. M. G. Pratt and B. E. Ashforth, "Fostering Meaningfulness in Working and at Work," in *Positive Organizational Scholarship*, ed. K. S. Cameron, J. E. Dutton, and R. E. Quinn (San Francisco: Berrett-Koehler, 2003), pp. 309–327.

14. Pratt and Ashforth, "Fostering Meaningfulness in Working and at Work."

15. Ibid.

16. S. Cranston and S. Keller, "Increasing the Meaning Quotient of Work," *McKinsey Quarterly* (Jan. 2013).

17. T. Schwartz, "The Twelve Attributes of a Truly Great Place to Work," *Harvard Business Review* Blog Network (Sept. 19, 2011).

18. B. Sanford, "The High Cost of Disengaged Employees," *businessjournal. gallup.com* (2013).

19. Staff of the Corporate Executive Board, "Involve Your Employees," *BloombergBusinessweek.com* (Dec. 11, 2009).

20. K. Kruse, "Why Employee Engagement?" *Forbes.com* (Sept. 4, 2012), citing *Employee Engagement at Double-Digit Growth Companies*, Hewitt Research Brief (2004).

21. Towers Watson Global Workforce Study (2012).

22. R. Wagner and J. K. Harter, *The Elements of Great Managing* (New York: Gallup Press, 2006).

23. "Comparative Annualized Stock Market Returns," greatplacetowork.com.

24. BlessingWhite Employee Engagement Research Update (Jan. 2013).

25. D. Claffey, "What Matters Most," *Enquirer* (June 16, 2013), p. s10.

26. M. Lagace, "How to Put Meaning Back into Leading," *HBS Working Knowledge*, hbswk.hbs.edu (Jan. 10, 2005).

CHAPTER 2: THE MARKERS OF MEANING

1. Based on annual survey data analyzed using Structural Equation Modeling (SEM), which runs hundreds of statistical models incorporating millions of data points from employees at a Fortune 100 company.

2. For all interviews conducted, the subject's title refers to the title they held at the time of the interview.

3. J. S. Bunderson and J. A. Thompson, "The Call of the Wild: Zookeepers, Callings, and the Dual Edges of Deeply Meaningful Work," *Administrative Science Quarterly* 54 (2009), pp. 32–57.

4. A. Wrzesniewski, C. McCauley, P. Rozin, and B. Schwartz, "Jobs, Careers, and Callings: People's Relations to Their Work," *Journal of Research in Personality* 31 (1997), pp. 21–33.

5. Wrzesniewski et al., "Jobs, Careers, and Callings."

6. Ibid.

7. S. H. Schwartz, "Universals in the Content and Structure of Values: Theory and Empirical Tests in 20 Countries," in *Advances in Experimental Social Psychology*, ed. M. P. Zanna, vol. 25 (New York: Academic Press, 1992), pp. 1–65.

8. Alan Alda quotes at www.goodreads.com.
9. W. Deresiewicz, "Don't Send Your Kid to the Ivy League," *NewRepublic.com* (July 21, 2014).
10. V. Gecas, "The Self Concept as a Basis for a Theory of Motivation," in *The Self-Society Dynamic: Cognition, Emotion, and Action*, ed. J. A. Howard and P. L. Callero (New York: Cambridge University Press, 1991), pp. 171–187.
11. Gecas, "The Self Concept as a Basis for a Theory of Motivation."
12. R. F. Baumeister and K. D. Vohs, "The Pursuit of Meaningfulness in Life," in *The Handbook of Positive Psychology*, ed. C. R. Snyder and S. J. Lopez (New York: Oxford University Press, 2002), pp. 608–618.
13. R. F. Baumeister and E. E. Jones, "When Self-Presentation Is Constrained by the Target's Knowledge: Consistency and Compensation," *Journal of Personality and Social Psychology*, 36 (1978), pp. 608–618, in S. J. Heine, T. Proulx, and K. D. Vohs, "The Meaning Maintenance Model: On the Coherence of Social Motivations," *Personality and Social Psychology Review* 10, no. 2 (2006).
14. Baumeister and Vohs, "The Pursuit of Meaningfulness in Life."
15. R. F. Baumeister, "The Self," in *Handbook of Social Psychology* (4th ed.), ed. D. T. Gilbert and S. T. Fiske, vol. 1 (New York: McGraw-Hill, 1998), pp. 680–740.
16. G. E. Kreiner, E. C. Hollensbe, and M. L. Sheep, "Where Is the 'Me' Among the 'We'? Identity Work and Search for Optimal Balance," *Academy of Management Journal* 49, no. 5 (2006), pp. 1031–1057.
17. B. D. Rosso, K. H. Dekas, and A. Wrzesniewski, "On the Meaning of Work: A Theoretical Integration and Review," *Research in Organizational Behavior* 30 (2010).
18. B. Ware, *The Top 5 Regrets of the Dying: A Life Transformed by the Dearly Departed* (London: Hay House, 2011).
19. C. J. G. Gersick, J. M. Bartunek, and J. E. Dutton, "Learning from Academia: The Importance of Relationships in Professional Life," *Academy of Management Journal* 43, no. 5 (2000), pp. 1026–1044.
20. H. Tajfel, M. Billig, R. P. Bundy, and C. Flament, "Social Categorization and Intergroup Behavior," *European Journal of Social Psychology* 1 (1971), pp. 149–177, in S. J. Heine, T. Proulx, and K. D. Vohs, "The Meaning Maintenance Model: On the Coherence of Social Motivations," *Personality and Social Psychology Review* 10, no. 2 (2006), pp. 88–110.
21. M. A. Hogg and D. J. Terry, "Social Identity and Self-Categorization Processes in Organizational Contexts," *Academy of Management Review* 25, no. 1 (2000), 121.
22. Hogg and Terry, "Social Identity and Self-Categorization Processes."
23. T. M. Welbourne, M. A. Cavanaugh, and T. A. Judge, "Does the Leader Make a Difference? Relationship Between Executive Leader Personality and Entrepreneurial Firm Performance," Center for Advanced Human Resource Studies (CAHRS), Working Paper series, 1998.

CHAPTER 3: THE POTENCY OF PURPOSE

1. A. Wrzesniewski, "Finding Positive Meaning in Work," in *Positive Organizational Scholarship*, ed. K. S. Cameron, J. E. Dutton, and R. E. Quinn (San Francisco: Berrett-Koehler, 2003).

2. A. Wrzesniewski, "It's Not Just a Job: Shifting Meanings of Work in the Wake of 9/11," *Journal of Management Inquiry* 11, no. 2 (2002), pp. 230–234.

3. A. M. Grant, "The Significance of Task Significance," *Journal of Applied Psychology* 93, no. 1 (2008), pp. 108–124.

4. V. Frankl, *Man's Search for Meaning* (Boston: Beacon Press, 1959), pp. 100–104.

5. E. Eaves, "America's Greediest Cities," *Forbes* (Dec. 3, 2007).

6. R. Albergotti, "The Most Inventive Towns in America," *Wall St. Journal* (July 2006), pp. 1, 22–23.

7. M. H. Immordino-Yang, "Reflection Is Critical for Development and Well-being," *Perspectives on Psychological Science* (July 5, 2012) pp, 358–359.

8. L. M. Ruehring, "Michelangelo Sculptures," www.entertainment.howstuffworks.com.

9. Oliver Wendell Holmes quotes at www.art-quotes.com.

10. "9 Basic Life Paths and Activities," manifestyourpotential.com.

11. E. A. Greenfield and N. F. Marks, "Formal Volunteering as a Protective Factor for Older Adults' Psychological Well-Being," *Journal of Gerontology, Social Sciences* 59B, no. 5 (2004).

12. www.muhammadaliquotes.org.

13. J. Collins and J. Porras, *Built to Last* (New York: HarperCollins 1994), p. 44.

14. Many thanks to Eric Breissinger for this great articulation.

15. M. Csikszentmihalyi, *Flow: The Psychology of Optimal Experience* (New York: Harper Perennial, 1990).

16. BlessingWhite Employee Engagement Research Update (Jan. 2013).

17. Grant, "The Significance of Task Significance," pp. 108–124.

18. J. Dutton, "Being Valued and Devalued at Work: A Social Valuing Perspective," in *Qualitative Organizational Research: Best Papers from the Davis Conference on Qualitative Research*, vol. 3 (Charlotte, NC: Information Age Publishing, 2012).

19. B. E. Ashforth and G. E. Kreiner, "How Can You Do It?" *Academy of Management Review* 24, no. 3 (1999), pp. 413–434.

CHAPTER 4: THE LIGHTHOUSE OF LEGACY

1. Evan Esar quote at www.quotationspage.com.

2. T. Maurer, "Start with Your Obituary," *Forbes.com* (Jan. 31, 2013).

3. "Directive #6: Leave a Legacy," www.thejanitorbook.com.

4. A. E. Winship, *Jukes-Edwards, A Study in Education and Heredity*, 1900 (Reprint Apr. 14, 2005, www.gutenberg.org).

5. Goethe quote at www.ranker.com.

6. *The Legacy Letters Project*, www.legacyletterproject.com.

7. K. Howe, *Iowa Alumni Magazine* (Aug. 2007).

8. Howe, "What I Know Now."

9. "From the Desk of Carol Alt," *The Legacy Letters Project*, www.legacyletterproject.com/carol_alt_8_7_06.pdf.

10. The Allianz American Legacies Study (Minneapolis: Allianz Life Insurance Co., 2005).

11. T. Rath, *Vital Friends*, Gallup (2011).

12. B. Ware, *The Top 5 Regrets of the Dying: A Life Transformed by the Dearly Departed* (London: Hay House, 2011).

13. P. Arnof-Fenn, "Leaving a Legacy," *Entrepreneur.com* (Dec. 15, 2006).

14. Charles de Lint quote at www.quotesdaddy.com.

15. *The Voisen Cooperative*, voisen.com.

16. B. Buford, *Halftime* (Grand Rapids, MI: Zondervan, 1994).

17. G. Weingarten, "Pearls Before Breakfast," *Washington Post* (Apr. 8, 2007).

18. Ibid.

19. Many thanks to Jacques Hagopian whose input helped crystallize the expression of my research/experience on this topic.

20. Rear Admiral Grace Murray Hopper quoted at womenshistory.about.com/od/quotes/a/gracehopper.htm.

21. M. Freedman, "When Retirees Misjudge Their Desire for Leisure," *blogs.wsj.com* (Apr. 2, 2014).

22. C. Flaman, "Focused Action = Exponential Results," in *Awakening the Workplace,* ed. A. Alfano, K. G. Scott, and M. Beth Page, (Canada: Experts Who Speak Books, 2006), pp. 23–24.

23. M. Beradino, "Mike Tyson Explains One of His Most Famous Quotes," www.articles.sun-sentinel.com (Nov. 9, 2012).

24. Sydney J. Harris, www.goodreads.com.

CHAPTER 5: LEARNING AND PERSONAL GROWTH

1. B. D. Rosso, K. H. Dekas, and A. Wrzesniewski, "On the Meaning of Work: A Theoretical Integration and Review," *Research in Organizational Behavior*, www.sciencedirect.com (October 2010).

2. Ray Stata quoted in A. Edwin and V. K. Jain, "Organizational Learning and Continuous Improvement," *The International Journal of Organizational Analysis* 3, no. 1 (Jan. 1995), pp. 45–68.

3. Brookings Institution study cited in K. M. Kapp, "Transforming Your Manufacturing Organization into a Learning Organization," *Hospital Materiel Management Quarterly* (June 1999) p. 1.

4. B. Boyd and J. Williams, "Developing Life-Long Learners Through Personal Growth Projects," *Journal of Leadership Education* 9, no. 2 (Summer 2010).

5. C. Tsay and M. R. Banaji, "Naturals and Strivers: Preferences and Beliefs About Sources of Achievement," *Journal of Experimental Social Psychology* (2011), pp. 2–5; cited in P. A. Murphy, "Beyond Talent and Smarts: Why Even Geniuses Struggle," *blogs.kqed.org* (Nov. 23, 2012).

6. G. Spreitzer and C. Porath, "Creating Sustainable Performance," *Harvard Business Review* (Jan.–Feb. 2012).

7. Carol Dweck cited in P. A. Murphy, "Eight Ways of Looking at Intelligence," *blogs.kqed.org* (June 10, 2013).

8. C. S Dweck and C. M. Mueller, "Praise for Intelligence Can Undermine Children's Motivation and Performance," *Journal of Personality and Social Psychology* 75, no. 1 (1998), pp. 33–52.

9. L. Donata, *Adult Learning: Understanding How Adults Learn*, http://education-teaching-careers.knoji.com/adult-learning-understanding-how-adults-learn.

10. J. Turner, "Social Media and Shrinking Attention Spans," www.myclever agency.com (Aug. 7, 2014).

11. D. Kolb, *Experiential Learning: Experience as the Source of Learning and Development* (Indianapolis: FT Press, 1983), cited in www.sierra-training. com.

12. *The Incredible Power of "Yet,"* www.greatschools.org/parenting-dilemnas/ 7539-parenting-tips-power-of-yet-carol-dweck-video.gs.

13. K. Leong, "Why You Shouldn't Have a Regular Exercise Routine," health mad.com/fitness (Aug. 18, 2009).

14. A. Wrzesniewski and J. Dutton, "Crafting a Job: Revisioning Employees as Active Crafters of Their Work," *Academy of Management Review* 26, no. 2 (2001), pp. 179–201.

15. J. K. Fletcher, Relational Practice: A Feminist Reconstruction of Work," *Journal of Management Inquiry* 7, no. 12 (1998), pp. 163–186.

16. R. C. Cohen and R. I. Sutton, "Clients as a Source of Enjoyment on the Job: How Hairstylists Shape Demeanor and Personal Disclosures," in *Advances in Qualitative Organization Research,* Ed. John A. Wagner (Greenwich, CT: JAI Press, 1998), pp. 1–32.

17. J. R. Hackman and G. P. Oldham, *Work Design* (Reading, MA: Addison-Wesley, 1980).

18. J. M. Berg, A. M. Grant, and V. Johnson, "When Callings Are Calling: Crafting Work and Leisure in Pursuit of Unanswered Occupational Callings," *Organization Science* 21, no. 5 (2010), pp. 973–994.

19. J. S. Bunderson, "The Call of the Wild: Zookeepers, Callings, and the Dual Edges of Deeply Meaningful Work," *Administrative Science Quarterly* 54 (2009), pp. 32–57.

20. Wrzesniewski and Dutton, "Crafting a Job," pp. 179–201.

21. Ibid.

22. E. Mitleton-Kelly, "What Are the Characteristics of a Learning Organization?" www.gemi.org/metricsnavigator/eag.

23. M. A. Gephart, V. J. Marsick, M. E. Van Buren, M. S. Spiro, and P. Senge, "Learning Organizations Come Alive," *Training & Development* 50, no. 12 (1996) pp. 35–45.

24. Kapp, "Transforming Your Manufacturing Organization into a Learning Organization."

25. D. Vanthournout, "Creating a High Performance Learning Environment: Seven Characteristics of High-Performance Learning," http://www. accenture.com/us-en/outlook/Pages/outlook-online-2011-creating-high-performance-learning-environment.aspx (Sept. 2011).

CHAPTER 6: MEANINGFUL DECISION MAKING AND INFLUENCE

1. R. F. Baumeister and K. D. Vohs, "The Pursuit of Meaningfulness in Life," in *The Handbook of Positive Psychology*, ed. C. R. Snyder and S. J. Lopez (New York: Oxford University Press, 2002), pp. 608–618.

2. Towers Watson Global Workforce Study (2012).

3. B. Steinheider, P. Bayerl, and T. Wuestewald, "The Effects of Participative Management on Employee Commitment, Productivity, and Community

Satisfaction in a Police Agency," paper presented at the annual meeting of the International Communication Association, Dresden International Congress Centre, Dresden, Germany, www.allacademic.com/meta/p93097_index.html.

4. B. Amble, "Empowering Leadership Not Always the Answer," www.management-issues.com/news/3679/empowering-leadership-not-always-the-answer (Oct. 16, 2006).

5. R. Hendren, "Involving Nurses in Shared Decision-Making," *HealthLeaders Media.com* (Feb. 2, 2010).

6. J. J. Gardiner, "Transactional, Transformational, and Transcendent Leadership: Metaphors Mapping the Evolution of the Theory and Practice of Governance," Kravis Leadership Institute *Leadership Review* 6 (2006), pp. 62–76.

7. Gardiner, "Transactional, Transformational, and Transcendent Leadership."

8. Many thanks to U.S. Army Ranger Patrick "Crossfit" Khattak for this great story.

9. *Journal of Personality and Social Psychology* cited in K. Salmansohn, "Bouncing Back: The Art (and Science)of Resilience," www.psychologytoday (June 30, 2011).

10. Y. Fried and G. R. Ferris, "The Validity of Job Characteristics Model," *Personnel Psychology* 40 (1987), pp. 287–322, in B. D. Rosso, K. H. Dekas, and A. Wrzesniewski, "On the Meaning of Work: A Theoretical Integration and Review," *Research in Organizational Behavior* 30 (2010) p. 97.

11. G. Spreitzer, "Taking Stock: A Review of More Than Twenty Years of Research on Empowerment at Work," in *The Handbook of Organizational Behavior,* ed. C. Cooper and J. Barling (Thousand Oaks, CA: Sage, 2007).

12. "Autonomy," www.referenceforbusiness.com.

13. M. McIntire, "How to Empower Employees to Make Effective Decisions on the Front-Line," imglv.com/articles/how_to_empower_employees.pdf (2011).

14. Ibid.

15. P. K. Mills and G. R. Ungson, "Reassessing the Limits of Structural Empowerment: Organizational Constitution and Trust as Controls," *The Academy of Management Review* 28, no. 1 (Jan. 2003), pp. 143–153.

16. Conrad Lashley, quote from an e-mail exchange.

17. L. Stack, "How to Empower Your Employees . . . and Yourself," the productivitypro.com/FeaturedArticles/article00134.htm (2009).

18. H. G. Halvorson, "How to Give Employees a Sense of Autonomy When You Are Really Calling the Shots," *Forbes.com* (Sept. 5, 2011).

19. E. Kain, "'Grand Theft Auto V' Crosses $1B in Sales, Biggest Entertainment Launch in History," *Forbes.com* (Sept. 20, 2013).

20. J. Fletcher, "5 Ways to Give Workers More Autonomy and Why It's Important," *blog.intuit.com/employees* (Dec. 26, 2012).

21. K. T. Dirks, L. L. Cummings, and J. L. Pierce, "Psychological Ownership in Organizations: Conditions Under Which Individuals Promote and Resist Change," in *Research in Organizational Change and Development*, ed. R. W. Woodman and W. A. Pasmore, vol. 9 (Greenwich, CT: JAI Press, 1996), pp. 1 23, cited in L. Van Dyne and J. L. Pierce, "Psychological Ownership and

Feelings of Possession: Three Field Studies Predicting Employee Attitudes and Organizational Citizenship Behavior," *Journal of Organizational Behavior* 25 (2004), pp. 439–459.

22. T. Farish, "Measuring Performance in the Workplace," www.techvibes.com/blog/measuring-performance-in-the-workplace-is-never-black-and-white, posted by Douglas Magazine (May 26, 2014).

CHAPTER 7: CULTURES OF CONSEQUENCE

1. D. Stewart, "Growing the Corporate Culture," in I. Younis Abu-Jarad, N. Yusof, and D. Nikbin, "Review Paper on Organizational Culture and Organizational Performance," *International Journal of Business and Social Science* 1, no. 3 (Dec. 2010) p. 26.

2. J. Kotter and J. Heskett, *Corporate Culture and Performance* (New York: Free Press, 1992).

3. SAS Company Information, www.sas.com/company.

4. T. B. Lawrence and S. Maitlis, "Care and Possibility: Enacting an Ethic of Care Through Narrative Practice," *Academy of Management Review* 37 (2012), pp. 641–663.

5. M. Conlin, "I'm a Bad Boss? Blame My Dad," *Bloomberg Businessweek* (May 9, 2004).

6. Warren Bennis cited in Conlin, "I'm a Bad Boss? Blame My Dad."

7. Brian DesRoches cited in Conlin, "I'm a Bad Boss? Blame My Dad."

8. C. Borchers, "Personal Touches Won Loyalty at Market Basket," *Boston globe.com* (July 25, 2014).

9. C. Ross, "Market Basket Vows to Replace Dissident Workers," *Bostonglobe.com* (July 31, 2014).

10. J. Bersin, "New Research Unlocks the Secret of Employee Recognition," *Forbes.com* (June 3, 2012).

11. C. Ventrice, *Make Their Day! Employee Recognition That Works* (San Franciso: Berrett-Koehler, 2009), p. 12.

12. "Baudville Peer to Peer Recognition," whitepaper, www.baudville.com/recognition-white-papers/rctypelisting/6/0/new, p. 1.

13. "Baudville Peer to Peer Recognition," p. 3.

14. J. Dutton, "Fostering High Quality Connections, *Stanford Social Review* (Winter 2003), pp. 54–57.

15. Bill Clinton story cited in B. Martinuzzi, "Degrees of Giving: Leading with Generosity," evancarmichael.com.

16. Towers Watson Global Workforce Study (2012).

17. Many thanks to Janette Yauch and Scott Richards for their leadership on this simplification initiative.

18. M. Kelly, *Off Balance, Getting Beyond the Work Life Balance Myth to Personal and Professional Satisfaction* (New York: Hudson Street Press, 2011).

19. Towers Watson Global Workforce Study (2012).

20. T. Schwartz, "The Productivity Myth," *Harvard Business Review* blog (May 5, 2010).

21. www.victorborge.org.

22. M. G. Pratt and B. E. Ashforth, "Fostering Meaningfulness in Working and at Work," in *Positive Organizational Scholarship*, ed. K. S. Cameron, J. E.

Dutton, and R. E. Quinn (San Francisco: Berrett-Koehler, 2003), pp. 309–327.

23. B. D. Rosso, K. H. Dekas, and A. Wrzesniewski, "On the Meaning of Work: A Theoretical Integration and Review," *Research in Organizational Behavior* 30 (2010), p. 109.

24. Ibid.

25. S. Intrator, "The Engaged Classroom," *Teaching for Meaning* 62, no. 1 (Sept. 2004), pp. 20–25.

26. D. Crim and G. Sejits, "What Engages Employees the Most, or the Top Ten C's of Employee Engagement," The Workplace, *Iveybusinessjournal.com* (Mar./Apr. 2006).

27. Pratt and Ashforth, "Fostering Meaningfulness in Working and at Work."

28. M. A. Hogg and D. J. Terry, "Social Identity and Self-Categorization Processes in Organizational Contexts," *Academy of Management Review* 25, no. 1 (2000), p. 121.

29. H. R. Markus and S. Kitayama, "Culture and the Self," *Psychological Review* 98, no. 2 (April 1991), pp. 224–253.

30. worthingtonindustries.com, media center—awards.

31. J. C. Maxwell, *Teamwork 101: What Every Leader Needs to Know* (Nashville: Thomas Nelson, 2008), p. 19.

32. Crim and Sejits, "What Engages Employees the Most."

33. A. Bruce, *Building a High Morale Workplace* (New York: McGraw-Hill, 2003), p. 10.

34. Q&A with Joel Podolny and Rakesh Khurana, in M. Lagace, "How to Put Meaning Back into Leading," *HBS Working Knowledge*, hbswk.hbs.edu (Jan. 10, 2005).

CHAPTER 8: MEANING-MAKING LEADERSHIP

1. M. G. Pratt and B. E. Ashforth, "Fostering Meaningfulness in Working and at Work," in *Positive Organizational Scholarship*, ed. K. S. Cameron, J. E. Dutton, and R. E. Quinn (San Francisco: Berrett-Koehler, 2003), pp. 309–327.

2. D. Ulrich and W. Ulrich, *The Why of Work* (New York: McGraw-Hill, 2010), p. xiv.

3. J. M. Podolny, R. Khurana, and M. Hill-Popper, "Revisiting the Meaning of Leadership," *Research in Organizational Behavior* 26 (2005), pp. 1–36, as cited in B. D. Rosso, K. H. Dekas, and A. Wrzesniewski, "On the Meaning of Work: A Theoretical Integration and Review," *Research in Organizational Behavior* 30 (2010), p. 101.

4. M. Rau-Foster, "Humor and Fun in the Workplace," workplaceissues.com.

5. L. Deutsch, "13 of Maya Angelou's Best Quotes," *USAToday.com* (May 28, 2014).

6. V. Kinjerski, "Employee Engagement: What Is an Employer or Employee Supposed to Do?" rethinkingyourwork.com (Feb. 5, 2010).

7. B. Shamir, R. J. House, and M. B. Arthur, "The Motivational Effects of Charismatic Leadership: A Self-Concept Based Theory," *Organization Science* 4, no. 4 (Nov. 1993), pp. 577–594.

8. Pratt and Ashforth, "Fostering Meaningfulness in Working and at Work."

9. T. B. Lawrence and S. Maitlis, "Care and Possibility: Enacting an Ethic of Care Through Narrative Practice," *Academy of Management Review* 37, no. 4 (2012), pp. 641–663.
10. P. Smith, *Lead with a Story* (New York: AMACOM, 2012).
11. T. Amabile and S. Kramer, "How Leaders Kill Meaning at Work," *McKinsey Quarterly* (Jan. 2012), www.mckinsey.com.
12. Charles Swindoll, www.goodreads.com.
13. M. Watkins, *The First 90 Days* (Boston: HBS Press, 2003), p. 13.

CHAPTER 9: CUTTING OFF CORROSIVE BEHAVIORS

1. S. J. Heine, T. Proulx, and K. D. Vohs, "The Meaning Maintenance Model: On the Coherence of Social Motivations," *Personality and Social Psychology Review* 10, no. 2 (2006), pp. 88–110.
2. M. G. Pratt and B. E. Ashforth, "Fostering Meaningfulness in Working and at Work," in *Positive Organizational Scholarship*, ed. K. S. Cameron, J. E. Dutton, and R. E. Quinn (San Francisco: Berrett-Koehler, 2003), pp. 309–327.
3. Heine et al., "The Meaning Maintenance Model."
4. D. Coughlin, "The Importance of Integrity," www.snowmagazineonline.com (May 31, 2012).
5. R. Thomas, "The Consequences of Leadership: Yes, Indecision IS a Decision," *TLNT.com* (July 1, 2013).
6. I. K. Schneider, "One Way and the Other: The Bidirectional Relationship Between Ambivalence and Body Movement," *Psychological Science* 24 (Mar. 2013), pp. 319–325, cited in J. Dean, "Sway: The Psychology of Indecision," Psyblog, www.spring.org.uk/2013/01/sway-the-psychology-of-indecision.php.
7. D. De Cremer, "Why Inconsistent Leadership Is Regarded as Procedurally Unfair: The Importance of Social Self-Esteem Concerns," *European Journal of Social Psychology* 33, no. 4 (July/Aug. 2003), pp. 535–550.
8. B. H. J. Schreurs, A. B. Bakker, and W. B. Schaufeli, "Does Meaning-Making Help During Organizational Change?" *Career Development International* 14, no. 6 (July 6, 2009), pp. 508–533.
9. J. Clemmer, "Mastering Change Through Continuous Growth, Learning, and Improvement," www.clemmergroup.com.
10. "Quotes of the Day: George Bernard Shaw on Connecting," www.news.investors.com (June 25, 2014).
11. S. Adkins-Green, "Seeing the Invisible Sign," blog.marykay.com (Apr. 16, 2012).
12. T. Amabile and S. Kramer, "How Leaders Kill Meaning at Work," *McKinsey Quarterly* (Jan. 2012), www.mckinsey.com.
13. Ibid.
14. J. Lopper, "How to Counteract Negativity in the Workplace," www.suite101.com (Oct. 22, 2013).

Index